THE VEST BOOK

THE
VEST BOOK

JACQUELINE FARRELL

With a foreword by Tom Gilbey

Create and customize
your own vests using
embroidery, fabric
painting, beadwork,
appliqué, and a host
of other techniques.

Chilton Book Company
Radnor, Pennsylvania

A QUARTO BOOK

Copyright © 1995 Quarto Inc.

Reprinted 1995

ISBN 0-8019-8648-6

A CIP record for this book is available
from the Library of Congress.

This book was designed and produced by
Quarto Inc.
The Old Brewery,
6 Blundell Street
London N7 9BH

Art editor Clare Baggaley
Designer Tanya Devonshire-Jones
Illustrator Jane Hughes
Photographer Laura Wickenden
Picture researcher Susannah Jayes
Senior editor Sally MacEachern
Editor Susan Baker
Art director Moira Clinch
Editorial director Sophie Collins

Typeset in Great Britain by
Central Southern Typesetters
Manufactured in Singapore by
Bright Arts Pte Ltd
Printed in Singapore by
Star Standard Industries (Pte) Ltd

CONTENTS

GALLERY
✵

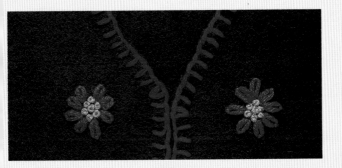

TECHNIQUES AND PATTERNS
✵

PUBLISHER'S NOTE

As far as the methods and techniques mentioned in this book are concerned, all statements, information, and advice given are believed to be true and accurate. However, neither the author, copyright holder, nor the publisher can accept any legal liability for errors or omissions.

BASIC SEWING EQUIPMENT
✵

For all the projects in this book, you will need the following basic sewing equipment in addition to the items mentioned in the individual Materials lists:

✵

- Handsewing needles
- Pins
- Scissors
- Tape measure
- Thimble

A sewing machine is not essential, but will obviously be an asset, especially if it will do machine embroidery.

FOREWORD

I HAVE ALWAYS HAD A PASSIONATE BELIEF IN THE VEST, OR WAISTCOAT, A SIMPLE GARMENT THAT HAS SURVIVED FOUR CENTURIES OF FASHION CHANGES. DATING BACK TO THE 1580s, THE BASIC DESIGN HAS HARDLY ALTERED, YET THE VEST REMAINS A VERSATILE GARMENT, SUITABLE FOR ANY OCCASION.

Evolving from its initial function as an undergarment, in the 1660s the vest made a revolutionary British fashion statement. It became a reaction to the traditional doublet and hose as well as the flamboyant French fashions. The English diarist, Samuel Pepys, frequently referred to the new garment in his diary of 1660. Writing of the British King Charles II, he said, "The King hath yesterday declared his resolution of setting a fashion for clothes which he will never alter. It will be a vest. I know not well how; but it is to teach the nobility thrift and will do good."

By contrast, Charles II's contemporary in France, Louis XIV, feeling snubbed by his action, initially relegated the vest, or waistcoat, to the lower classes. However, it was not long before he adopted it, dandifying the garment in the process by introducing richly embroidered fabrics and precious stones.

By 1825, Charles II's vision of the vest reappeared again, but less "peacock" and more functional. It was not, however, until the latter part of the nineteenth century, when color virtually disappeared from men's wardrobes, that traditional woolen checks and plaids became popular, coinciding with the sobriety that was emerging as an integral characteristic of men's fashion. This theme lasted until the reaction to the austerity of post-war Britain, when in the late 1940s men once again displayed their vest-ial plumage.

TOM GILBEY

My own interest in the vest goes back over 25 years, to when I first opened my couture house. I recognized that this simple garment served the purpose of a jacket, but without the restrictions that sleeves sometimes impose. Noting that it had been as much a favorite with the cowboys of the last century as with twentieth-century rock guitarists – both requiring their arms to be unencumbered for easy access to the tools of their trade – I became excited with the idea of developing the vest further, bringing it up-to-date to meet the needs of today's wearers, from office-bound professionals and dandies displaying their colors at night to outdoor activists such as bikers, cyclists, skaters, etc., who need uncluttered, dual-purpose garments offering warmth and practicality.

Today's modern manufacturing techniques, laser printing devices, and performance fabrics allow the vest to fit into any background as well as to suit all price brackets. Professionals, socialites, rock stars, and construction workers alike now have a means of expressing their individual style while still meeting the functional demands of their profession and pocket!

JACQUELINE FARRELL

The vest has a great past and a very varied personality, and looks forward to a terrific and versatile future. Crossing all social boundaries, the vest is to the '90s what the T-shirt was to the '60s.

Tom Gilbey

CUSTOMIZING VESTS

THE CLASSICAL SCROLLS OF THE ROCOCO PERIOD IN DESIGN AND ARCHITECTURE ARE RECREATED ON THIS VEST USING READY-MADE GOLD CORD IN TWO THICKNESSES TO GIVE ADDED TEXTURE.

ROCOCO VEST

✶ ✶ ✶ ✶ ✶ ✶ ✶ ✶ ✶ ✶ ✶ ✶ ✶ ✶ ✶ ✶ ✶

MATERIALS
✶

- Basic sewing equipment
- 2¼ yards gold cord, ¼-inch thick
- 2¼ yards gold cord, ⅛-inch thick
- Gold colored sewing thread
- Cellophane tape

✶ **TIP** *To create an interesting contrast, the couching thread could be a different color or an unusual texture.*

1 Cut both the thick and thin cord in half and wrap tape around the raw ends to prevent fraying. The thick cord will form the core of the design. The thin cord is used for the smaller scrolls.

2 Lay the unbuttoned vest on a flat surface. Pin one sealed end of one length of the thick cord inside the right neckline. Pin the other end under the front peak, then lay the cord in swirls and waves down the front of the vest. Experiment with the design at this stage. The cord will curl easily, allowing manipulation. When you have a layout you are happy with, pin it in place.

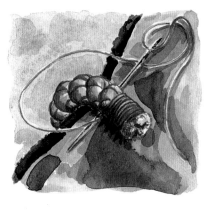

3 Thread the needle with gold sewing thread and begin by oversewing the raw end of the thick cord underneath the lower edge of the vest after removing the tape carefully. Keep the stitches close together to form a "satin stitch" bar. This will secure the end and keep it looking neat.

4 The cord is "couched" onto the surface. Do this by stitching over and under it, through the vest, keeping the stitches evenly spaced about ⅛ inch apart. Continue up the front, finishing at the neck with a "satin stitch" bar on the inside to cover the raw end.

5 Place the thin cord in scrolls at various angles to the main line, cutting suitable lengths. Begin at the lower half of the vest front. Gently push a raw end of the thin cord between the thick cord and the vest fabric. Pin it in place and sew a few stitches to secure it. Carefully trim off any excess cord that is showing through, then pin the length into a small scroll. Trim the excess cord and wrap all ends in tape.

6 Couch the scroll in place, securing raw ends underneath the cord itself. Repeat small scrolls all the way up the front of the vest, varying the length of the cord and the tightness of the coil to create added interest. Repeat for the other side.

THIS FUN VEST ALLOWS YOU TO RECYCLE NOT ONLY AN OLD VEST, BUT ALSO ALL THOSE

LOOSE BUTTONS THAT YOU KNEW YOU WOULD FIND A USE FOR SOMEDAY!

RAINBOW BUTTON VEST

❋ ❋ ❋ ❋ ❋ ❋ ❋ ❋ ❋ ❋ ❋ ❋ ❋ ❋ ❋ ❋

MATERIALS
❋

- Basic sewing equipment
- Assorted buttons (approx. 300)
- 4½ yards rickrack in a bright color
- Strong button thread
- Sewing thread to match braid
- Tailor's chalk

1 Sort all the loose buttons into groups according to color: reds, greens, blues, pearl, etc. You can either plan your button pattern in advance, or let it develop as you go along.

2 Lay the unbuttoned vest on a flat surface. Using tape measure and tailor's chalk, mark a line 1 inch from all the edges on the front of the vest.

You can either remove the fastening buttons to apply the braid, then stitch them on top, or stitch the braid alongside the buttons.

3 Cut the rickrack into 2¼-yard lengths. Begin by folding one raw end under and pin it to the front edge of the right shoulder seam ½ inch in from the edge of the neckline. Pin the braid all the way around the right front panel, following the chalk line.

4 When you reach the buttonholes, snip the braid and fold the ends through the top and bottom of the buttonholes. Pin them in place. The braid can be hand stitched using backstitch, or machine stitched using straight or zigzag stitch. Trim the pockets if required.

Finish off by tucking the raw end under at a side seam. Repeat for left side.

❋ TIP *Lightweight plastic buttons without shanks are best for this project as they will lie flat, although you can use a mixture.*

5 Once the braid is in place, you can begin to sew on the buttons. Thread the needle with the strong button thread and arrange a small group of buttons on the bottom left area of the vest front. Sew on the buttons, starting with the end of the thread securely knotted and finishing on the back by overcasting. Cover all of the left side of the vest in this way.

6 Repeat step 5 on the right side. You could create a contrasting pattern by building up stripes of color, or spell out a name or initials to personalize your vest.

☼ **TIP** *If the vest becomes very heavy in front, you may need to sew light dressmaking weights into the back lining to prevent the front from drooping.*

VANILLA ROSEBUDS AND DUSTY PINK SATIN FABRIC WORK WELL TOGETHER ON THIS ROMANTIC-
LOOKING VEST. ALL YOU HAVE TO DO IS SOME HAND SEWING.

RIBBON ROSE SATIN VEST

✿ ✿ ✿ ✿ ✿ ✿ ✿ ✿ ✿ ✿ ✿ ✿ ✿ ✿ ✿ ✿ ✿

1 Divide the large and small roses into two equal groups, one for each side of the vest. Lay the vest on a flat surface and arrange the roses on it to experiment with the design.

MATERIALS
✿

- Basic sewing equipment
- 36 (approx.) medium cream ribbon rosebuds
- 36 (approx.) small cream ribbon rosebuds
- Thread to match rosebuds

2 In the vest pictured here, the rosebuds have been randomly scattered around the border, but a more formal design would work equally well. When you have achieved an arrangement that you are happy with, pin each rosebud in place.

3 Thread the needle and knot the end of the thread. Insert the needle from the back behind the rose nearest to the shoulder seam, preparatory to working down each front. Bring the needle through to the front, then insert it through the base of the rosebud. Bring the needle down through the fabric to complete the stitch, then repeat twice to secure the rose.

4 To continue, carry the thread across the reverse of the vest and bring the needle up at the next rose. Stitch it in place.

5 If the roses are scattered widely, begin and end each rose with a knot and overcasting. Do not carry the thread across large areas on the reverse as long threads may snag or break and will look unsightly.

6 Continue down each vest front in turn until complete. For a truly delicate look, you could sew rosebuds on instead of the existing buttons.

BOLD SHAPES AND COLORS COMBINE TO MAKE THIS VEST EQUALLY SUITABLE FOR ADULTS OR CHILDREN. THE MAIN TECHNIQUE USED IS HAND EMBROIDERY.

EXOTIC EMBROIDERED VEST

MATERIALS

* Felt squares in the following colors: pink, purple, yellow, lime, green
* Stranded floss: two skeins each of lime and turquoise
* Crewel needle No. 4
* Scissors
* Felt-tip pen
* 8 x 10-inch tracing paper
* 20-inch square fusible web
* 8 x 10-inch lightweight cardboard
* Iron

1 Using the pen and tracing paper, trace one of each of the templates below: square, triangle, flower, and center. Trace the shapes onto cardboard and cut out. Once trimmed, your templates are ready to use.

2 First lay the square on the paper side of the fusible web and trace around it eight times, keeping the shapes close together to save waste. Cut out the areas traced, and place them bonding side down on the pink felt. Using a hot iron, bond them to the felt. Cut around the shapes. Repeat for the remainder of the shapes and colors. Remove paper backing.

TEMPLATES

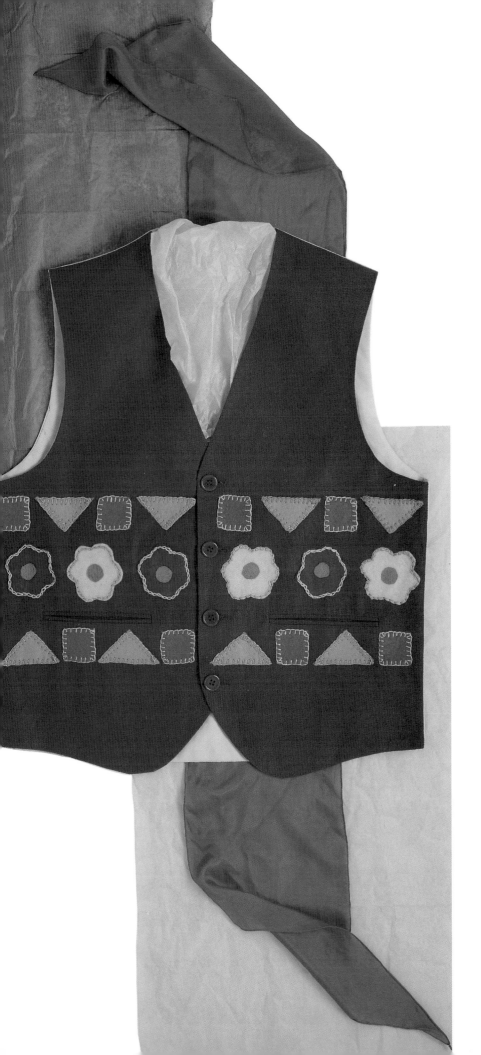

3 Lay the vest on a flat surface. Place the felt motifs bond side down on the vest. Using a hot iron, bond the motifs in place. The heat may take a while to penetrate through the felt, so repeat as necessary but do not allow fabric to burn. A damp cloth placed over the design during pressing will help prevent burning.

4 Thread the needle with an 18 inch length of lime stranded floss. Use all six strands. Begin either with a knot or catch the loose end under the reverse of the first few stitches. Start with a pink square and work open buttonhole stitch (see Stitch Glossary). Finish by running the end under the reverse of the last few stitches. Use the lime thread around the pink squares and turquoise thread around the triangles.

5 Thread the needle with lime floss. Begin as directed in step 4, but work chain stitch around the outside edge of the purple flowers (see Stitch Glossary). Use the turquoise thread to work chain stitch around the yellow flowers. The green centers are left unembroidered, but will remain in place due to the fusible web. When the embroidery is complete, press lightly, using a dry cloth on the front and reverse of the vest.

STENCILING IS AN EXCITING AND EASY METHOD OF CUSTOMIZING A VEST. THE COLORS CAN BE AS SOFT OR AS INTENSE AS YOU WISH, AND THERE IS ENDLESS SCOPE FOR CREATING DIFFERENT DESIGNS.

TULIP STENCIL VEST

MATERIALS

- 3 medium-soft stencil brushes
- 1 fine soft paint brush
- Stencil paint – sunflower yellow, scarlet, pine green
- Paper towel
- Thin glazed white cardboard or acetate film, 5 x 8 inches
- Large sheet of medium-weight cardboard
- Pencil
- Craft knife
- Tracing paper
- Masking tape
- Pins
- Glass jars

TIP *If you make a* small *mistake with the paint, dabbing with masking tape* may *remove it.*

1 Stretch and pin one of the vest fronts onto the cardboard, making sure the fabric is quite taut. This will prevent it from moving when stenciling.

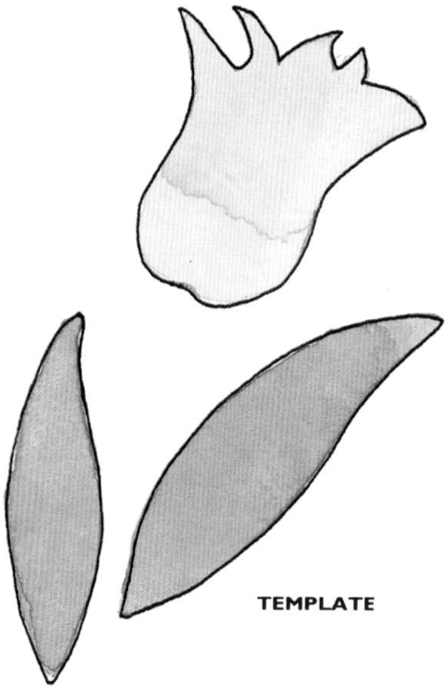

TEMPLATE

2 Trace the stencil design on tracing paper and rub it down onto white cardboard or acetate. Carefully cut out the design using a craft knife.

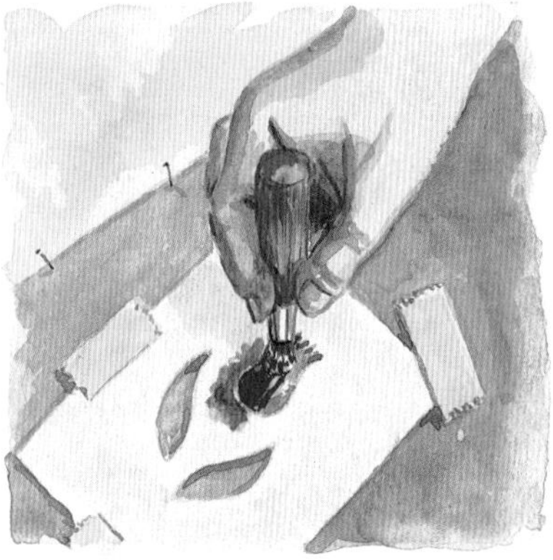

3 Prepare stencil paint as directed by the manufacturer (each product is different). Creme paints were used here. Lay the tulip-head stencil on top of the vest. Anchor it in place with masking tape or stencil fixative. Dip a brush into the scarlet paint and dab it on a paper towel to remove excess paint. Hold the brush perpendicular to the stencil and apply the paint in either a sweeping or circular motion, from the base of the tulip almost to the top. You can repeat the process if you want a deeper color.

4 Dip a *clean* brush into the sunflower yellow paint and begin filling the stencil from the top of the flower head, blending the color as you go. Use the fine brush dipped in the yellow paint to add purer color and highlights. This will complete the tulip head.

Remove the stencil, lay it on a paper towel and rub lightly with a clean paper towel to remove excess paint.

5 Replace the stencil on the fabric and position the leaves. The stencil has been designed so that you can add leaves at various angles to make each flower totally individual. Tape the stencil in place. Dip a clean brush into the pine green paint and fill each leaf shape with the green. Using the yellow stencil brush, stroke down from the point of each leaf to add lighter highlights. More detail can be applied using the fine brush with yellow paint.

6 The brushes and stencil can be cleaned with paper towels during stenciling, but should be cleaned after use with liquid detergent and warm water, or as directed by the manufacturer. For further information on stenciling see pages 98–101.

GLITTERING BUGLE BEADS AND SEED PEARLS ADD GLAMOUR TO A PLAIN WHITE VEST.
THE DESIGN WOULD BE EQUALLY EFFECTIVE ON A BLACK BACKGROUND.

BEADED SUNBURST VEST

✸   ✸   ✸   ✸   ✸   ✸   ✸   ✸   ✸   ✸   ✸   ✸   ✸   ✸   ✸   ✸   ✸   ✸

TEMPLATES

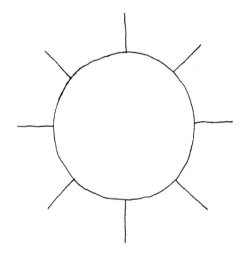

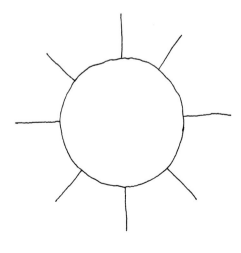

1 Trace the templates (left) for each sun, then lay them on a light box or tape them to a window pane. Place the vest on top and mark it with a water soluble pen. Alternatively, trace the circular shapes, trim around them, lay them on the vest, and mark around them with tailor's chalk.

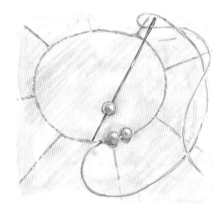

2 Thread a beading needle and knot the end of the thread. Bring the thread up from the reverse of the fabric to the front, at the edge of a small sun. Slide a seed pearl on the needle and insert the needle into the fabric. Use two stitches to secure the bead. Work around the circle edge attaching the seed pearls.

MATERIALS

✸

- Basic sewing equipment
- 1 packet of ¼-inch gold bugle beads
- 1 packet of ¹⁄₁₂-inch seed pearls
- 1 packet of ¹⁄₁₆-inch circular beads in assorted colors
- Beading needles
- Strong fine white thread
- Air/water soluble pen, or tailor's chalk

BEADING LAYOUT

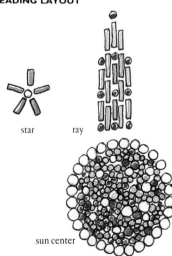

star   ray

sun center

3 Stitch the sun center with an assortment of seed pearls and circular beads, to create an interesting texture.

4 To make rays for the sun, follow the diagram (left). Remember to stitch each bead twice to secure it in place. Each sun should have eight rays about 1½ inches long. Work the large sun in the same way as the small sun.

5 To make the stars, sew seed pearls on randomly, but evenly spaced, all over each front.

6 Surround each pearl with five bugle beads as shown in the diagram (left). You can make as many or as few stars as you wish. Fasten off and trim the threads after sewing each star. It is best not to carry the threads across the back of the vest. For further information on beading, see pages 96–7.

ARTIFICIAL FUR PROVIDES A FUN ALTERNATIVE TO THE REAL THING AND IS EASY TO SEW.
USE OUR COLLAR PATTERN TO TRANSFORM A PLAIN VEST INTO SOMETHING MORE GLAMOROUS.

FUN FUR VEST

❋ ❋ ❋ ❋ ❋ ❋ ❋ ❋ ❋ ❋ ❋ ❋ ❋ ❋ ❋ ❋ ❋

1 Trace the collar pattern as directed in the techniques section on pages 114–15. Lay the fur fabric on a flat surface with the pile facing toward you. Fold the right sides together, using just enough to lay the collar pattern on easily. Pin the pattern in place. Cut around the pattern through the fur. Repeat the process for the lining.

2 Pin the collar pieces right sides together, at the short edge. This should be marked on the pattern piece. Baste, then stitch them together on the machine using a straight stitch.

The stitches should be set at length ³⁄₁₆ inch for this project to allow for the depth of the pile. (The tension will need to be adjusted as well. Refer to the machine handbook.)

Press the seam open with a medium-hot iron and a dry pressing cloth.

Repeat all these stages with the lining, adjusting the stitch length and tension as necessary.

3 Pin, baste, and stitch the fur collar to the lining, placing right sides together. Pin the outside edge of the collar all the way around; then baste and stitch. Trim off excess bulk from the seam allowance at the collar seam, then snip small triangular areas from the edge seam allowance at regular intervals. Snip *close to*, but *not on*, stitching line. This will mean the curved edge sits flat when turned right side out.

Turn the collar right side out, press, and topstitch the seam about ³⁄₁₆ inch from edge. This will also help the collar to lie flatter.

MATERIALS
❋

- Basic sewing equipment
- 20 inches of 20-inch wide fur fabric (here, leopard print)
- 2¼ yards of ¾-inch wide cream bias binding (or background color of vest)
- 20 inches of 45-inch wide lining in cream (or background color of vest)
- Cream (or matching) sewing thread
- ¾-inch self-cover buttons (as required)
- Dressmaking shears
- Sewing machine
- Iron
- Pressing cloth

❋ **TIP** *To avoid sewing mistakes, practice on a scrap of fur fabric first, trying out different stitch lengths and tensions.*

4 Use bias binding to attach the collar to the vest. Turn under ¾ inch and press the raw end of the bias binding. Pin the edge of the binding to the raw edge of the collar through both fur layer and lining. Pin and baste all the way along the binding fold, then stitch the raw end under. Machine stitch in place.

5 Pin the combined edge of the bias binding and collar to the inside edge of the vest collar. Baste, then hand sew them together. To hold the loose end of the binding, catch it with a few hand stitches at the ends and at intervals along the inside.

6 To cover the buttons, trim circles of fur ³⁄₁₆ inch larger than the button cover. Cover the button and fold excess fur to the inside, making sure there are no bumps or folds around the edge. Snap on the back plate of the button and sew it in place of a regular button.

THE SUMPTUOUS DECORATION ON THIS VELVET VEST REQUIRES A STEADY HAND AND SUBTLE COLOR CHANGES TO ACHIEVE MAXIMUM EFFECT.

BAROQUE VELVET VEST

✿ ✿ ✿ ✿ ✿ ✿ ✿ ✿ ✿ ✿ ✿ ✿ ✿ ✿ ✿ ✿ ✿

1 First choose your design. Bear in mind that it must work both as a repeat design and as a mirror image. You can enlarge or reduce your design on a photocopier to fit the size of the vest, or use the grid method shown on pages 118–9.

2 Place cardboard between the front and back of the vest. To keep the vest in place, stick it down firmly with masking tape. Transfer the design to tracing paper with chalk. Place the tracing, chalk side down, on the vest and anchor it firmly in position with masking tape.

3 Using a pencil, carefully rub over the back of the tracing. It is very important to make sure that the tracing does not slip or the pattern will blur as it is transferred to the vest. Check at intervals that the chalk is adhering to the velvet; you need a precise line for an ornate design. Gently remove the tracing paper.

4 Paint from top to bottom in one direction. You can either work on one area and let it dry completely or move to a completely separate area where there will be no danger of smudging your previous work. For best results, hold the paint nozzle slightly above the fabric and rest your wrist on a firm surface.

MATERIALS
✿

- Tracing paper
- White chalk
- Pencil
- Masking tape
- Scissors
- Cardboard
- Liquid embroidery paints in bronze, silver, and gold

WITH IMAGINATION AND FLAIR, YOU CAN COMPLETELY TRANSFORM A PURCHASED VEST BY COVERING IT WITH RIBBONS, PATCHES, AND AN ASSORTMENT OF FOUND OBJECTS RANGING FROM A CHILD'S TOY TO SHELLS. IT IS GREAT FUN TO MAKE, AND THE RESULT WILL BE ENTIRELY ORIGINAL IN APPEARANCE.

MAD, MAD VEST

✺ ✺ ✺ ✺ ✺ ✺ ✺ ✺ ✺ ✺ ✺ ✺ ✺ ✺ ✺ ✺ ✺

MATERIALS
✺

- Basic sewing equipment
- Ruler
- Tailor's chalk
- Fabric patches – selection of colors and textures: printed cotton, satin, lace, metallic cloth
- Ribbons – selection of different widths and colors
- Found objects, such as children's small toys, crackerjack prizes, shells, beads, bells or squeakers – anything that can be sewn or glued
- Glue
- Sewing machine (optional)

1 Use the ruler and chalk to mark a grid of diamonds or rectangles on the vest. The chalk lines indicate where to sew the ribbon and also outline the areas for fabric patches or found objects.

2 Cut patches of fabric to fit neatly into some of the boxes or areas created by the grid. Pin the patches in place and try on the vest to make sure that the arrangement looks reasonably well balanced. You should also take the found objects into consideration (see step 5).

3 When all the fabric patches have been pinned, sew on the ribbons either by hand or by machine. It is important to make sure that the ribbon is stitched to the vest fabric and that it covers the raw edges of the fabric patches to keep them in place and to prevent them from fraying.

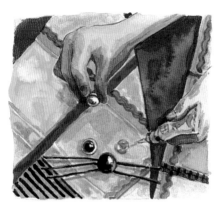

4 Turn the ends of the ribbon under at the edges of the vest. Two sets of ribbons could be extended at the waist across the back to make a tie. A good way to finish off free ribbon ends is to roll and sew the edges and attach tiny rocaille beads to hide the seam.

5 Arrange the found objects. Make sure that they are sewn or glued on firmly. Some items, such as the squeaker behind the teddy bear patch, may have to be put in position at an earlier stage. You can use anything you like to create a unique, personalized garment.

6 If the existing buttons are plain or dull, you could change them for something more exciting, such as these candy-tube caps which are simply glued onto self-cover buttons.

THIS PROJECT IS QUICK AND EASY, AND VERY FLEXIBLE. SIMPLY BY USING A PIECE OF FLORAL PRINTED FABRIC AND SOME FUSIBLE WEB, YOU CAN CREATE NUMEROUS DESIGN COMBINATIONS ON THE VEST OF YOUR CHOICE.

FLORAL APPLIQUÉ VEST

❉ ❉ ❉ ❉ ❉ ❉ ❉ ❉ ❉ ❉ ❉ ❉ ❉ ❉ ❉ ❉

MATERIALS
❉

- Basic sewing equipment
- 45-inch wide floral printed fabric (approx. 1 yard depending on design and final application)
- 20 inches fusible web
- Iron
- Pressing cloth

1 Choose the areas that you wish to use from your printed fabric. Points to note are: Is the design well defined? Are the proportions correct for the size of vest? Can more than one image be used from the design: roses, buds, leaves, garlands?

2 Cut the fusible web into small pieces to match your chosen design areas. Lay them on the reverse of the fabric, bonding side down, and press with a medium-hot iron on the paper side. Trim around each motif and the web. Continue until you have a selection of motifs.

3 Lay the vest on a flat surface. Place the motifs on the vest and experiment with proportions, arrangements, and color combinations. At this stage the design can be made as simple or as complicated as you choose.

4 When you have made your final selection, peel off the backing paper, place each bonded motif back down, and pin in position. When all the motifs are placed, press with a medium-hot iron and, if required, a damp pressing cloth.

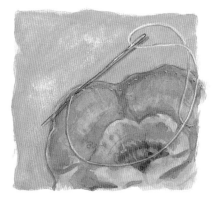

5 To make sure the motifs are permanent and can stand wear and tear, it is best to stitch around each one using stab stitch. Knot the thread and bring the needle up from the back. Then insert the needle just behind the point where it emerged, take it through to the back, and bring it up again a short distance to the left of the first stitch.

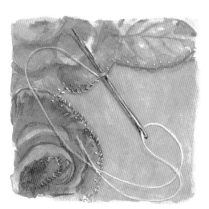

6 Make the next stitch as before and repeat the process around the motif. The result is a line of tiny dots around the edge of the motif and a neat line of stitches on the reverse. Finish by oversewing neatly. Repeat for all motifs.

MAKING VESTS

THIS VEST WAS INSPIRED BY THE COLORS AND MOTIFS IN TRADITIONAL **AMERICAN** QUILTING.

A CLASSIC RAW SILK FABRIC IN CREAM PROVIDES A PERFECT FOIL FOR THE RASPBERRY AND

SCARLET HEARTS SURROUNDED BY DELICATE TENDRILS AND SAGE LEAVES. **F**USIBLE WEB AND

MACHINE EMBROIDERY MAKE THE INTRICATE DESIGN QUICK AND EASY TO EXECUTE.

SWEETHEART VEST

✿ ✿ ✿ ✿ ✿ ✿ ✿ ✿ ✿ ✿ ✿ ✿ ✿ ✿ ✿ ✿ ✿ ✿

TEMPLATES

1 Cut up the fusible web into small pieces similar in size to the scraps of colored fabric. Trace the outlines of the templates onto the paper backing of the bonding. Make as many of each shape as you need to decorate your vest. Iron each piece of bonding to its corresponding scrap of fabric. Cut out each shape with small, sharp scissors.

✿ **TIP** *Before starting this project, use some scrap material to try out the suggestions in the machine embroidery techniques section.*

MATERIALS

✿

- Basic sewing equipment
- 1 yard cream raw silk, 45 inches wide
- 1 yard fusible interfacing 45 inches wide
- 1⅔ yards cream lining, 45 inches wide
- 18 inches fusible web
- 5 × ¾-inch self-cover buttons
- Rayon machine embroidery thread in jade and turquoise
- Basting thread (dark)
- Sewing thread to match the lining
- Scraps of silk in raspberry, scarlet, sage
- Sewing machine
- Dressmaking scissors
- Embroidery scissors
- Embroidery hoop (medium)
- Vest pattern
- Dark tailor's chalk

2 Lay the silk fabric right side up on a flat surface. Find the center of the fabric by folding it in half, selvage to selvage, then mark it with pins.

3 Place the front vest pattern piece right side up on the right side of the fabric, with the front opening edge lying along the center of the fabric. Pin it in place. Mark the dart, then draw all around the edge with tailor's chalk. Reverse the pattern piece and repeat for the other half.

4 Baste around the chalk outlines. Using tailor's chalk, mark the seam allowances inside the outline. Your design should not go beyond these seam lines. Do *not* cut the panels out at this stage.

5 Peel the paper backing from the bonded shapes and lay them glue-side down onto each vest panel. Attach them in place using a medium-hot iron.

6 Using the embroidery designs (right) as a guide, draw embroidery guidelines onto the fabric using tailor's chalk. Try to vary the designs on adjacent hearts and leaves, and use scrolls of different sizes.

7 Start the embroidery by placing the bottom left corner of the panel in an embroidery hoop, making sure that the fabric is held taut. This will prevent the material from puckering when you are embroidering.

8 Thread the sewing machine with the jade thread for the top thread, filling the bobbin with the turquoise thread. Set both the stitch width and stitch length to zero and detach the presser foot.

9 Slip the hoop under the needle arm and position it so that the fabric lies flat against the bed of the machine. *Lower* the presser foot lever to activate the tension spring.

10 With the presser foot removed, there is no automatic feed, so the length of the stitches will depend on how heavily you press on the power pedal and how quickly you move the fabric. Start slowly at first, then gradually increase your speed, working in a continuous, fluid movement.

11 Move the hoop around the fabric to complete both vest panels, making sure the fabric is always held taut. Remove the fabric from the machine from time to time to get an idea of how the overall design is developing.

12 Pull all trailing threads to the reverse of the fabric; knot and trim them. Press the fabric lightly on the wrong side to iron out any puckers. Cut out the panels and make the vest as described on pages 108–11.

WITH A BASIC KNOWLEDGE OF KNITTING STITCHES, YOU CAN CREATE THIS BRIGHT FUN VEST

WITH INDIVIDUAL FRINGING AND JAZZY BUTTONS.

SUNFLOWER KNIT VEST

✿ ✿ ✿ ✿ ✿ ✿ ✿ ✿ ✿ ✿ ✿ ✿ ✿ ✿ ✿ ✿ ✿

Instructions are given for the first size, with larger size(s) given in square brackets [ ]. Where only one figure is given, it applies to all sizes.

Gauge
22 sts and 30 rows to 4 in (stockinette st) on No. 6 needles or size needed to achieve stated gauge.

MATERIALS
✿

- Double knitting in sunflower yellow (see chart for quantity)
- Double knitting in lime and tangerine for tassels
- 7 fruit buttons
- No. 3 knitting needles
- No. 6 knitting needles
- Large tapestry needle
- Crochet hook
- Scissors

Measurements
To fit bust/chest

32	34	36	38	40	42	44	46	inches

Actual size

35½	38	40	42	44	45½	48	50	inches

Finished length

20½	21	21¼	21½	22½	23	23½	24	inches

Quantities
Double knitting

5	5	6	6	6	7	7	7	2-ounce balls

Quantities of yarn are approximate as they are based on average requirements.

✿ **TIP** *It is important to check your gauge before starting your garment. If there are too many stitches to 4 in, your gauge is tight and you should change to larger needles. If there are too few, your gauge is loose and you should change to smaller needles.*

Abbreviations

alt=alternate; **beg**=beginning; **cont**=continue; **dec**=decrease by working 2 sts together; **foll**= following; **in**=inches; **inc**=increase by working into front and back of st; **K**=knit; **M1**=make a st by picking up horizontal loop lying before next st and working into back of it; **meas**=measures; **P**=purl; **patt**= pattern; **rem**=remain; **rep**=repeat; **RS**=right side; **stockinette st**=1 row K, 1 row P; **st(s)**=stitch(es); **tog**= together.

Tw2R=K into front of second st on left needle, then K into front of first st and slip both sts off needle together.

Tw2L=K into back of second st on left needle, then K into front of first st and slip both sts off needle together.

Cr2R=K into front of second st on left needle, then P into front of first st, slipping both sts off needle together.

Cr2L=P into back of second st on left needle, then K into front of first st, slipping both sts off needle together.

Before starting to knit, read the instructions carefully and circle all figures relating to your size with a colored pencil.

Cable panel patt (14 sts)
Row 1 – (RS), P3, Tw2L, P4, Tw2L, P3.
Row 2 and every alt row – K all K sts and P all P sts.
Row 3 – P3, K2, P4, K2, P3.
Row 5 – P3, Tw2L, P4, Tw2L, P3.
Row 7 – (P2, Tw2R, Tw2L) twice, P2.
Row 9 – P2, K3, Tw2L, Tw2R, K3, P2.
Row 11 – P2, Cr2L, K2, Tw2R, K2, Cr2R, P2.
Row 13 – P3, Cr2L, Tw2R, Tw2L, Cr2R, P3.
Row 15 – P4, Tw2L, K2, Tw2L, P4.
Row 17 – P3, (Tw2R, Tw2L) twice, P3.
Row 19 – P2, (Tw2R, K2) twice, Tw2L, P2.
Row 21 – P2, K3, Cr2R, Cr2L, K3, P2.
Row 23 – (P2, Cr2L, Cr2R) twice, P2.
Row 24 – K all K sts and P all P sts.
These 24 rows form cable panel patt.

Left front

With No. 3 needles, cast on 42 [**44**, 46, **50**, 52, **54**, 58, **62**] sts.
Rib row 1 – (RS), *K1, P1; rep from * to last 2 sts, K2.
Rib row 2 – *K1, P1; rep from * to end.
Rep these 2 rows for 2¾in, ending with row 1.
Inc row – Rib 1 [**2**, 2, **3**, 2, **3**, 2, **1**], *M1 (**by picking up horizontal loop lying before next st and working into back of it**), rib 10 [**8**, 7, **9**, 8, **8**, 11, **15**]; rep from * to last 1 [**2**, 2, **2**, 2, **3**, 1, **1**] sts, M1, rib to end. (47 [**50**, 53, **56**, 59, **61**, 64, **67**] sts).

Change to No. 6 needles and **patt, placing cable panel patt** thus:
Row 1 – (RS), K12 [**15**, 18, **21**, 24, **26**, 29, **32**], cable panel patt 14 sts as row 1, K21.
Row 2 – P21, cable panel patt 14 sts as row 2, P12 [**15**, 18, **21**, 24, **26**, 29, **32**].
These 2 rows **set** patt.

Cont in patt as set **working appropriate rows of panel patt** until left front meas 11 in (or adjust to suit), ending with RS facing for next row.

Shape armhole and front slope
Next row – Bind off 3 sts, patt to end.
Work 1 row.

Next row – K2tog, patt to last 2 sts, K2tog.
Next row – Patt to last 2 sts, P2tog.
Next row – K2tog, patt to end.
Next row – Patt to last 2 sts, P2tog.

Dec 1 st as before at armhole edge on next and every foll alt row, **at the same time** dec 1 st as before at front edge on next and every foll 4th row until 34 [**33**, 34, **36**, 37, **38**, 41, **41**] sts rem, ending with RS facing for next row.
Dec 1 st as before at front edge **only** on every foll 4th row from previous dec until 23 [**22**, 23, **25**, 26, **27**, 29, **29**] sts rem.
Work straight until left front meas 20½ [**21**, 21½, **21½**, 22½, **23**, 23½, **24**] in, ending with RS facing. Bind off.

Right front
With No. 3 needles, cast on 42 [**44**, 46, **50**, 52, **54**, 58, **62**] sts.
Rib row 1 – (RS), K2, *P1, K1; rep from * to end.
Rib row 2 – *P1, K1; rep from * to end.
Rep these 2 rows for 2¾ in, ending with row 1.
Inc row – Rib 1 [**2**, 2, **3**, 2, **3**, 2, **1**], *M1, rib 10 [**8**, 7, **9**, 8, **8**, 11, **15**]; rep from * to last 1[**2**, 2, **2**, 2, **3**, 1, **1**] sts, M1, rib to end. (47 [**50**, 53, **56**, 59, **61**, 64, **67**] sts).
Change to No. 6 needles and **patt, placing cable panel patt** thus:
Row 1 – (RS), K21, cable panel patt 14 sts as row 1, K12 [**15**, 18, **21**, 24, **26**, 29, **32**].
Row 2 – P12 [**15**, 18, **21**, 24, **26**, 29, **32**], cable panel patt 14 sts as row 2, P21.
These 2 rows **set** patt.
Work to match left front reversing shapings, working an extra row before armhole shaping and shoulder bind off.
Back
With No. 3 needles, cast on 85 [**91**, 95, **103**, 107, **113**, 119, **125**] sts.
Rib row 1 – (RS), K1, *P1, K1; rep from * to end.
Rib row 2 – P1, *K1, P1; rep from * to end.

Rep these 2 rows for 2¾ in, ending with row 1.

Inc row – Rib 8 [**4**, 8, **3**, 6, **8**, 4, **7**], *M1, rib 5 [**6**, 5, **7**, 6, **7**, 8, **8**]; rep from * to last 7 [**3**, 7, **2**, 5, **7**, 3, **6**] sts, M1, rib to end. (100 [**106**, 112, **118**, 124, **128**, 134, **140**] sts).
Change to No. 6 needles and **patt, placing cable panel patt** thus:
Row 1 – (RS), K12 [**15**, 18, **21**, 24, **26**, 29, **32**], cable panel patt 14 sts as row 1, K48, cable panel patt 14 sts as row 1, K12 [**15**, 18, **21**, 24, **26**, 29, **32**].
Row 2 – P12 [**15**, 18, **21**, 24, **26**, 29, **32**], cable patt 14 sts as row 2, P48, cable patt 14 sts as row 2, P12 [**15**, 18, **21**, 24, **26**, 29, **32**].
These 2 rows **set** patt.
Cont in patt as set **working appropriate rows of panel patt** until back matches fronts to start of armhole shaping, ending with RS facing for next row.
Shape armholes
Keeping patt correct, bind off 3 sts at beg of next 2 rows.
Dec 1 st at each end of next 5 rows, then on every alt row until 80 [**80**, 84, **88**, 92, **94**, 100, **102**] sts rem.

Work straight until back matches fronts to shoulder bind off, ending with RS facing for next row.
Shape shoulders
Cast off 23 [**22**, 23, **25**, 26, **27**, 29, **29**] sts at beg of next 2 rows. Bind off rem 34 [**36**, 38, **38**, 40, **40**, 42, **44**] sts.

Make up
Omitting ribbing, press lightly following instructions on the ball band. Join shoulder seams.

Armhole borders
With RS facing and No. 3 needles, pick up and knit 135 [**143**, 147, **155**, 167, **171**, 179, **183**] sts evenly all round armhole edge.
Starting with row 2, work in rib as on back for 7 rows. Bind off in rib.

Border
With No. 3 needles, cast on 9 sts.
Row 1 – (RS), K2, (P1, K1) 3 times, K1.
Row 2 – K1, (P1, K1) 4 times.
Rep these 2 rows until border, when slightly stretched, fits up left front for woman/right front for man to start of front slope shaping, sewing in place as you go along.
Mark position of 7 buttons on border with pins to ensure even spacing, first to come ⅝ in up from lower edge, last to come ⅝ in below start of front slope shaping and remainder spaced evenly between.
Cont in rib up left front slope for woman/right front slope for man, around back neck, down right front slope for woman/left front slope for man, then down to lower edge, with the addition of 7 buttonholes to correspond with pins on border, sewing in place as you go along.
Bind off in rib.

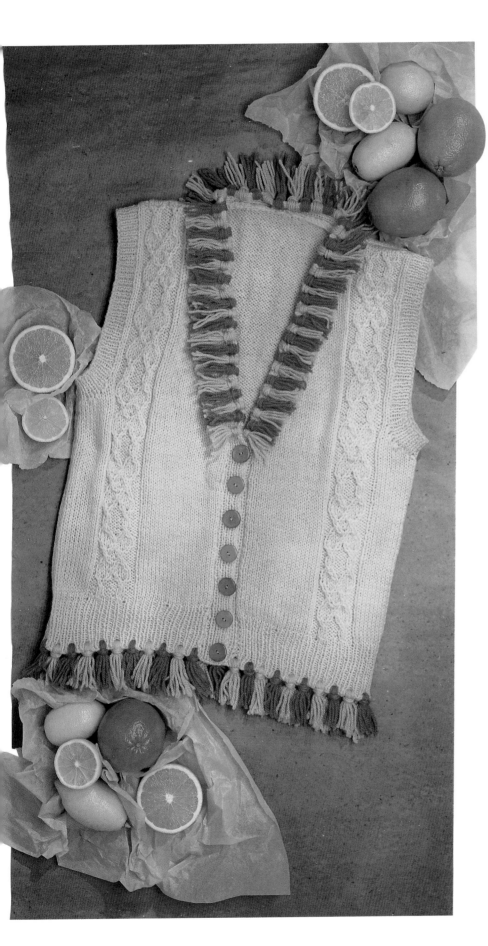

To make a buttonhole:
(RS), rib 4 for woman/3 for man, bind off 2, rib to end and back, casting on 2 over bind off stitches.

Join side seams and armhole borders.
Sew on buttons.

Fringing

To complete the vest add the tassels. Each tassel consists of 5 strands of yarn 6 in long. Alternative tassels can be made with lime and orange yarn. The amount required will vary depending on the finished size of the vest.

Begin the fringing on the right front at the buttonhole band and right front rib seam. Attach the tassels using a crochet hook. Insert the hook underneath the right front and four rows up. Push the hook through to right side, wrap five strands over the hook and pull through to underneath.

Draw loose ends over the front of the vest, then through the loop, and tighten.

Place a tassel every second rib alternating colors, continue around back and left front, finishing at left front buttonhole band. Repeat the process for the neckband tassels and trim ends even.

GOLDEN CHERUBS CARRYING HEARTS ALOFT DECORATE THIS SILK VEST WHICH WOULD BE APPROPRIATE FOR A WEDDING. THE CHERUBS ARE MACHINE EMBROIDERED.

CHERUB WEDDING VEST

❈ ❈ ❈ ❈ ❈ ❈ ❈ ❈ ❈ ❈ ❈ ❈ ❈ ❈ ❈ ❈ ❈

1 Trace the cherub template (right) onto tracing paper.

2 Bond the gold dupion silk to the fusible web with an iron.

4 Reverse the cherub template and trace the cherub again on the remaining fabric.

3 Lay the tracing on a light box or tape it to a window. Place the silk paper-side down on top and mark it with a soluble pen.

5 Using the vest template given on pages 120–1, make a paper pattern. Lay the pattern on the cream dupion, pin and baste around the edge. Mark darts. Remove the pattern, then reverse and repeat.

6 Cut roughly around each cherub shape, then trim it neatly to within 1/16 inch of the outline.

7 Peel off the paper backing and lay each cherub with the hearts facing to the center. The feet should begin about 4 inches up from the edge of each peak and 1 1/2 inches in from the edge. The bottom wing should be slightly above the top dart marking. Press each cherub in place.

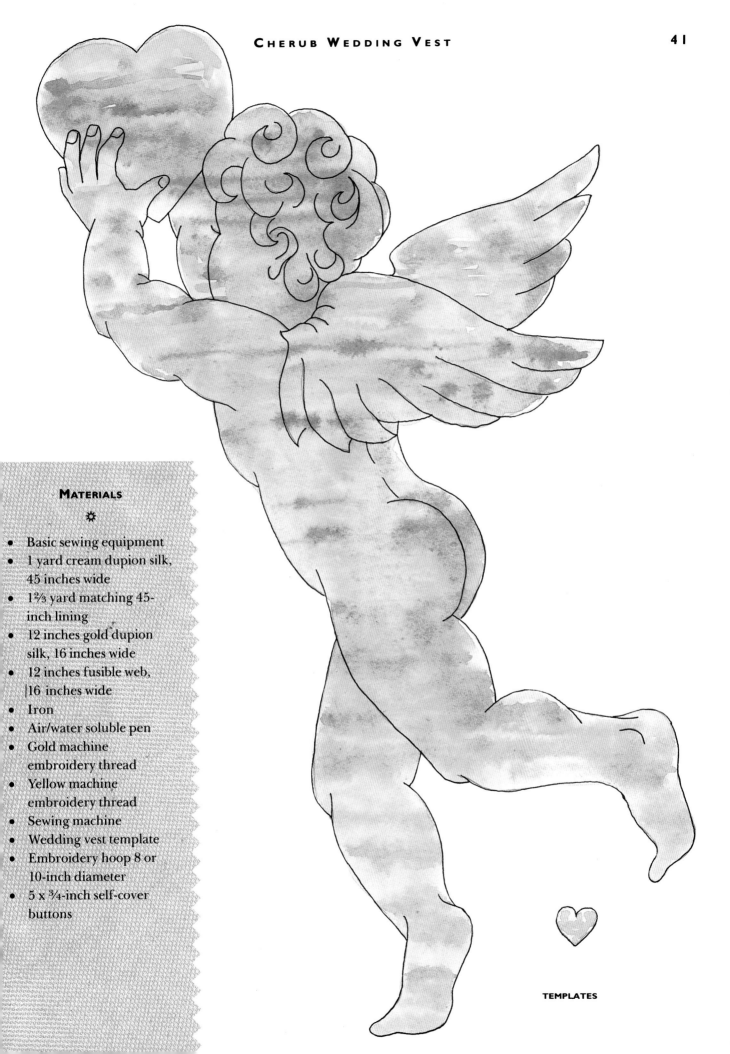

MATERIALS
☼

- Basic sewing equipment
- 1 yard cream dupion silk, 45 inches wide
- 1⅔ yard matching 45-inch lining
- 12 inches gold dupion silk, 16 inches wide
- 12 inches fusible web, 16 inches wide
- Iron
- Air/water soluble pen
- Gold machine embroidery thread
- Yellow machine embroidery thread
- Sewing machine
- Wedding vest template
- Embroidery hoop 8 or 10-inch diameter
- 5 x ¾-inch self-cover buttons

TEMPLATES

8 Set up the machine to do free-style embroidery according to the machine's handbook (or see pages 94–5). The stitch length should be zero, the stitch width zero, the presser foot removed, and the feed dog down or covered with a darning plate. A darning foot can be used if required. The gold thread should be used as the top thread with the bobbin filled with yellow thread. *Lower* the presser foot bar to activate the tension. Practice first on a scrap of fabric stretched in a hoop. The stitches should be close together.

9 When you feel confident with your machine embroidery stitching, move on to the vest. Stretch the design taut in the hoop and lower the needle to begin on a top wing. Stitch slowly and carefully around all the lines marked, going over lines twice, or even three times, to achieve a strong image.

10 Carry the threads across to different areas of the design when required. You can trim them afterwards; they should not unravel if the stitches are kept very close together.

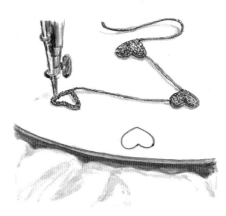

11 Using scraps of cream dupion, trace the heart template and embroider it using the gold thread, filling the shape. Leave about 2 inches between each motif. You will find it helpful to use an embroidery frame.

12 Finish by pressing the design with a damp cloth and a steam iron. Assemble as directed on pages 108–11.

13 Cover buttons by cutting out the heart motifs, making circles slightly larger than the button. Cover each button, keeping the motif central, and snap on the back plate. Sew on the buttons.

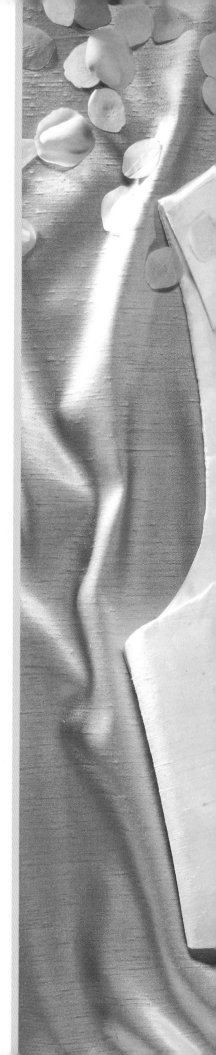

THIS WARM, COLORFUL VEST IS HAND-EMBROIDERED USING BRIGHT TAPESTRY YARN. ONLY
THREE DIFFERENT STITCHES ARE NEEDED TO CREATE THE DESIGN, WHICH IS INSPIRED BY
TRADITIONAL MEXICAN EMBROIDERY.

MEXICAN FELT VEST

✿ ✿ ✿ ✿ ✿ ✿ ✿ ✿ ✿ ✿ ✿ ✿ ✿ ✿ ✿ ✿ ✿

MATERIALS
✿

- Basic sewing equipment
- ¾ yard green felt fabric, 45 inches wide
- Tapestry yarn in orange, yellow, raspberry, jade (one skein of each) and scarlet (two skeins)
- Crewel needle size 3 or 4
- Scissors (dressmaking and embroidery)
- Iron
- Tailor's chalk or bright basting thread
- Green sewing thread
- Sewing machine (optional)

1 Trace the pattern given for the Mexican felt vest on pages 122–3. Lay the felt on a flat surface. Place the paper pattern, right side up, close to the lower right-hand corner. (Do not place it exactly at the corner as each front panel will need a little extra fabric to allow it to fit easily into the embroidery hoop at the edge of the design.) Pin the pattern in place and mark the outline with tailor's chalk or basting thread. Reverse the pattern piece and repeat for the other side.

2 Trim roughly around the two marked front panels to make this stiff fabric a more manageable size for embroidery.

3 Fold the remainder of the fabric in half and place the back pattern piece on the fold. Pin it in place, mark the outline with chalk and cut around the back panel. Set it aside.

4 Mark the position of the first flower on each side by measuring 2 inches up and 2 inches from the inside corner of each front. Use tailor's chalk or a contrasting basting stitch.

☼ **TIP** *For an alternative look, you could embroider the floral motif around the edge only, or you could embroider simple leaf and stem shapes between the flowers.*

5 Now that the first flower center has been established, mark the other flower centers, which should all be approximately 3 inches apart.

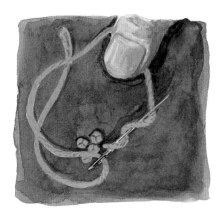

6 The flowers are worked in alternate colorways: jade and orange, then yellow and raspberry.

Thread the needle with jade yarn 18 inches in length. Knot the end of the yarn, or secure it under the first few stitches for a neater finish on the reverse. Bring the needle through to the surface at the first dot marked, hold the yarn down using the left thumb, and encircle the needle twice with the yarn as shown.

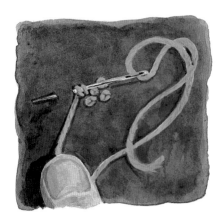

7 Continue to hold the yarn taut while you twist the needle over and insert it close to where the yarn first emerged. As you pull the yarn through to the back, the loops of yarn around the needle will create a French knot.

8 Move on to the position of the next stitch. Each flower center has seven French knots. Secure the yarn on the reverse by sliding the needle under a few stitches. Trim loose ends.

9 Use daisy stitch to work the petals. Thread a needle with the appropriate color, secure the yarn on the reverse, and bring the needle up at the top of the cluster of French knots. Holding the yarn down with your left thumb, insert the needle next to the point where the yarn emerged, then bring the point out ⅜ inch away.

10 Pass the point over the loop of yarn and tighten it slightly to create a rounded petal shape. One tiny stitch over the end of the loop secures it. Repeat this around the central French knot cluster to form eight petals in total.

11 Once all motifs have been completed on each panel, cut out the pattern pieces. To join the fronts and back, stitch at the shoulder seams and sides using either straight stitch on a sewing machine or backstitch if you are sewing by hand. Press open the seams. There is no need to overlock the seams as the felt should not fray.

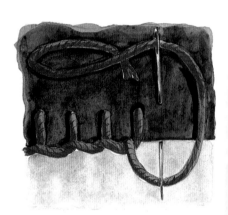

12 To give a decorative finish, overcast the edges in detached buttonhole stitch (blanket stitch) using the scarlet yarn. Begin on the lower edge at one of the side seams. Bring the thread out on the lower edge, insert the needle again on the reverse at a position ⅜ inch up, taking a straight downward stitch with the yarn under the needle point. Pull the yarn through the loop and repeat making the next stitch a short distance away.

13 The looped edge should follow the edge of the cut shape. Work around all the edges including armholes. Press to finish.

THE COLORS OF THE SEA, SHELLS, AND SAND COMBINE TO MAKE THE BACKGROUND FOR THIS STUNNING CRAZY PATCHWORK VEST. STARFISH, WAVES, AND SHELL SHAPES FORM THE BASIS OF THE MOTIFS.

SEASHORE PATCHWORK VEST

1 Enlarge the ladies' vest pattern on pages 118–19. Scale up the templates noting which thread and pattern to use on each, following the key diagram (right).

2 Lay out the antique gold silk and trace the vest fronts using either a fabric pen or chalk, or a running stitch. Mark darts clearly. Allow 2 inches around the pattern. This will allow you to fit it securely into the embroidery hoop. Lay the paper templates for the areas marked 1 on top of the gold fabric and mark each area, according to the diagram.

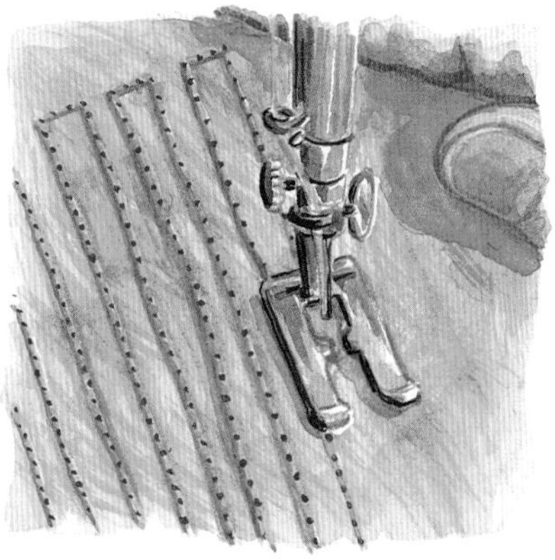

3 To embroider, set machine for straight stitch using the colored threads as directed on the diagram. The bottom tension should be set slightly looser than normal for all the embroidery in this project. Do this by slackening the small screw on the bobbin case very slightly. Practice on a scrap of fabric first. When the tension is correct, the finished effect is of a main top thread dotted with "sparks" of color from the bobbin. Remove the presser foot and *lower* the presser foot bar.

Fill all areas marked 1 with straight lines ¼ inch apart.

4 Mark the template shapes for areas 2 on the pink fabric. Leave a margin 2 inches from outside edge to allow fabric to fit into the hoop.

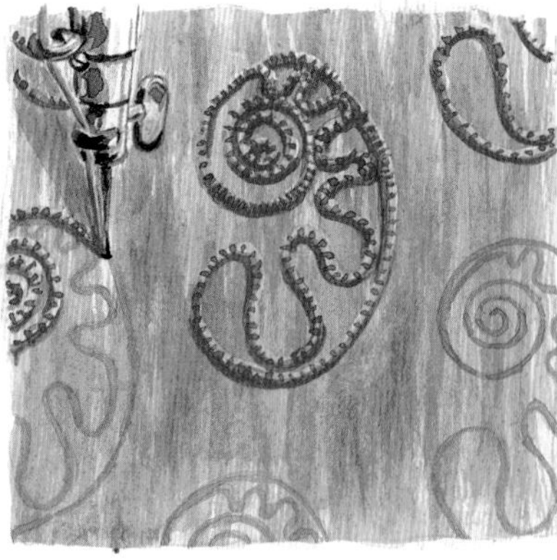

5 Trace the shell motifs onto the fabric using a vanishing fabric marker or chalk.

MATERIALS

☀

- Basic sewing equipment
- 1⅛ yards antique gold dupion silk, 47 inches wide
- ½ yard bronzed pink dupion silk, 47 inches wide
- ½ yard glacier blue dupion silk, 47 inches wide
- ½ yard green shot (turquoise/gold) dupion silk, 47 inches wide
- 1⅔ yards white silk lining, 47 inches wide
- 30 inches fusible web
- Assorted spools of machine embroidery thread
- Machine embroidery hoop 8 or 10-inch diameter
- Scissors: dressmaking and embroidery
- Iron
- 5 × ¾-inch self-cover buttons
- Sewing machine
- Buttonhole thread in white
- Basting thread *or* tailor's chalk/fabric pen

MATERIALS GUIDE

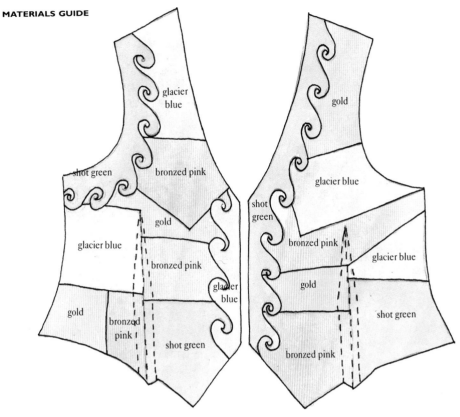

THREADS GUIDE

1 golden yellow top thread
hot pink bottom thread

2 golden yellow top thread
bronze bottom thread

3 turquoise top thread
moss green bottom thread

4 tangerine top thread
pale shell pink bottom thread

5 moss green top thread
turquoise bottom thread
(reverse for 5b)

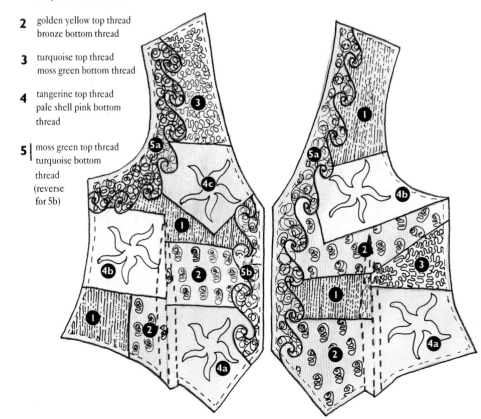

6 Always use a hoop, as the finished result will be of a better quality. To do free embroidery, remove the presser foot from the machine and *lower* the feed dog. This will allow you to practice free embroidery first, as directed in the techniques on pages 94–5. Thread the machine with the correct colors as shown on the diagram on page 49. *Lower* the presser foot bar. Start at the center and spiral around 3 or 4 times, then drop down 1 inch before sewing a wavy line back to the top.

7 Mark the templates on the blue fabric for areas 3, leaving a 2-inch hoop allowance as before. Thread up according to the chart. Embroider the vermicelli pattern as shown on the diagram on page 49. There is no need to trace it, as the charm of this motif is its irregularity.

8 Mark the templates for areas 4a, 4b, and 4c, onto the appropriate fabric. Trace the starfish design using a fabric pen.

9 Put the fabric into the hoop, set the machine with the correct colored threads, and begin by outlining the starfish, then fill in with spirals of varying size and density.

10 Trim each embroidered panel and then iron them onto the fusible web. Pin each in place before ironing them onto the gold base fabric.

11 Return all machine settings to straight stitch: attach the presser foot, raise the feed dog, reset the bobbin tension to normal, and set the stitch length for 2 or 3. Sew around each patchwork piece using the correct harmonizing thread; i.e. blue for glacier blue, bronze for bronzed pink, etc.

12 Cut out templates for areas 5a and 5b – the "waves." Iron on the fusible web, then pin and bond them in place according to the diagram on page 49. The fabric will now be quite stiff so you may not need a hoop. Reset the machine for free embroidery using the thread according to the chart and fill in the waves with a continuous spiral.

13 You should now have two completed front vest panels. Make as directed on pages 108–11.

14 Cover five buttons in gold fabric embroidered with straight lines and sew them onto the vest front.

EDGE-STITCHED SCALLOPS AND A SIMPLE CUTWORK DETAIL MAKE THIS DELICATE VEST PERFECT TO WEAR WITH A SUMMER DRESS.

SIMPLE SUMMER VEST

✿ ✿ ✿ ✿ ✿ ✿ ✿ ✿ ✿ ✿ ✿ ✿ ✿ ✿ ✿ ✿ ✿ ✿

MATERIALS
✿

- Basic sewing equipment
- 1½ yards white cotton lawn 36 inches wide
- White cotton sewing thread
- Scissors (embroidery and dressmaking)
- Sewing machine
- Iron
- Tailor's chalk or air/water soluble pen
- Stitch-and-tear interfacing, 30 × 30 inches
- 4 yards white or contrasting bias binding (optional)

Cutwork motif with four distance marks. Use these to space your pattern correctly.

1 Using the cutwork vest pattern on pages 122–3, trace the front and pin onto fabric; mark around edge with tailor's chalk or pen. Reverse the front pattern and mark around it for the other front piece.

Fold the fabric and lay the back pattern piece against the fold. Pin and mark around it. Cut out the pieces.

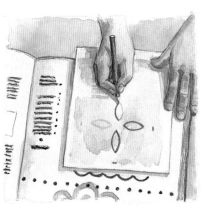

2 Trace the cutwork motif (left) onto tracing paper, including distance marks.

3 Lay the motif on a light box or tape it to a window. Place the vest fabric over it, beginning in the bottom right-hand corner of the front right-hand side. The motif should begin ¾ inch from the seam allowance of ⅝ inch.

4 Trace the motif onto the fabric using the chalk or pen. Do not trace the distance marks.

5 Move the vest along to trace each motif. For each new motif, the distance mark should line up with the tip of the last petal drawn on the last motif. Each front should have six motifs.

6 Once the motifs have been traced onto the fabric, pin the interfacing in place on the reverse of the motifs. This will create a stiffer fabric on which to sew and will overcome the problem of the fabric pulling or stretching.

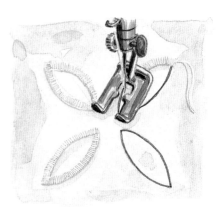

7 To begin a motif, set the machine up with white cotton thread on top and bottom and set the control for zigzag stitches. The shorter the stitch *length* set, the closer together each stitch will be, creating a satin stitch. (Practice on a scrap of fabric first.) Work around each petal shape, finishing by leaving 2-inch thread ends which should be pulled through to the reverse of the design, knotted, and trimmed once all the motifs have been stitched.

10 To make the vest, set the machine for normal straight stitch. Pin the vest wrong sides together at the shoulder side and seams. Baste, then stitch them taking a seam allowance of ⅝ inch. Press the seams open and overcast the raw edges using an evenly spaced zig-zag stitch to prevent fraying.

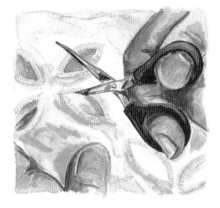

8 Using small sharp scissors, trim away the center of each motif very carefully.

9 Gently tear off the interfacing from the reverse of the fabric.

11 To finish this vest, set the machine for scallop stitch if it has this control; otherwise, mark a scallop detail around the edge using tailor's chalk and the template on page 52. Stitch over this line using satin stitch.

The scallop details should be worked ½ inch away from the raw edge to prevent pulling. Trim away excess fabric. Press the finished vest.

☼ **TIP** *To create a transparent effect, repeat the motif at regular intervals all over the front panels.*

12 Alternatively, trim the edges with matching or contrasting bias binding all around the edge and the armholes.

THIS WONDERFUL DESIGN CAN BE CREATED USING FABRIC PAINT AND SALT! DETAIL IS ADDED USING A GOLD OUTLINER TO CREATE THE EFFECT OF LOOKING UNDERWATER.

GREEN AND GOLD AQUATIC VEST

❊ ❊ ❊ ❊ ❊ ❊ ❊ ❊ ❊ ❊ ❊ ❊ ❊ ❊ ❊ ❊ ❊

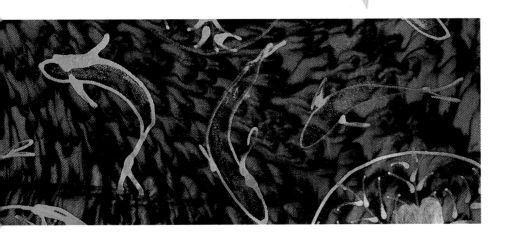

MATERIALS
❊

- 36 × 36 inches white silk twill (plus scraps for testing)
- 60 inches black lining fabric 45 inches wide
- Selection of paint brushes (very fine to 1½ inch)
- Table salt
- Iron
- Wooden stretcher frame 35 × 35 inches approx.
- Thumbtacks
- Deep green silk fabric paint
- Gold silk outliner pen

2 Cover your work surface with newspaper to protect it and lay the frame on it fabric side up.

1 Stretch the fabric on the frame, holding it in place with thumbtacks. Make sure it is taut, as it will stretch when wet with paint.

❊ **TIP** *If you have never done fabric painting before, test the steps on scraps of fabric first.*

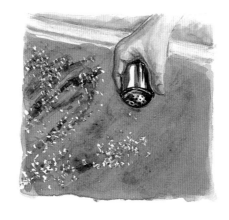

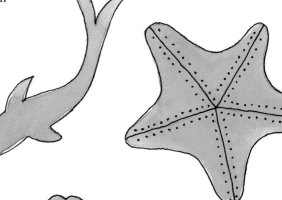

4 While the paint is still wet, sprinkle small quantities of table salt over it. This will absorb and disperse the paint, creating an unusual background effect.

3 Dip a large brush into the green paint and paint on the silk in bold strokes, working fairly quickly. Do not worry about getting the paint even, as varied depths of color will create a more interesting texture.

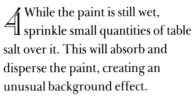

TEMPLATES

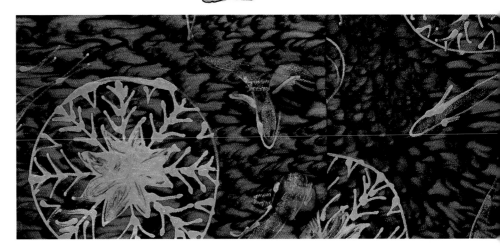

5 Leave the fabric to dry, then shake the salt off. The length of time it takes to dry will depend on how wet you have made the fabric.

6 Remove the fabric from the frame, and iron carefully using the "silk" setting, or a steam iron. The heat will "fix" the paint, but take care not to damage the silk.

7 Re-stretch the fabric on the frame, pinning it into position as before.

10 Repeat the motifs at random all over the fabric until you achieve the desired effect. Leave it to dry. The gold paint is alcohol-based, so it does not need heat to fix it. If you wish to iron the silk again, iron it on the back.

11 Remove the painted fabric from the frame and make it into a vest, following the instructions on pages 108–11. For further information on fabric painting, see pages 98–101.

8 Begin to draw a design with the gold outliner pen (see Tip).

9 Fish and abstract water lilies have been used here, but you could choose starfish, shells, seaweed, or seahorses.

✿ TIP *If you do not feel confident about tackling the gold outline freehand, try cutting cardboard stencils traced from images in magazines or from the motifs shown. Even a simple repeated circle would work well against this textural background.*

BRIGHT COLORS AND DISTINCTIVE STAMP MOTIFS COMBINE TO MAKE THIS UNUSUAL STRIPED
VEST. SATIN STITCH EMBROIDERY IN GOLD HIGHLIGHTS EACH STRIPE.

STARS AND STRIPES VEST

✸ ✸ ✸ ✸ ✸ ✸ ✸ ✸ ✸ ✸ ✸ ✸ ✸ ✸ ✸ ✸ ✸

1 Make a vest pattern as shown on pages 118–19. Fold the fabric in half and lay the vest pattern at the open edge (not the fold). Trace the shape and cut out the two front panels. Trace and cut out the back panel and lay it aside.

2 Tape the fabric onto a flat surface, then mark the stripes. Begin 2½ inches up from the point of the vest, then lightly draw a horizontal line in pencil.

3 Continue to mark lines at the following intervals for both fronts: 1st 2½ inches from front point; 2nd 1 inch; 3rd 4 inches; 4th 1 inch; 5th 3 inches; 6th 1 inch; 7th 4 inches; 8th 1 inch; 9th 3 inches; 10th 1 inch.

4 Use the large star stamp and the green ink pad to fill in areas marked A as shown on the diagram (right). Press the stamp lightly on the pad. Do not overload it with ink. Press it firmly onto the fabric, but be careful not to move the stamp as this will smudge the image.

MATERIALS
☀

- Basic sewing equipment
- 28 inches white cotton, 36 inches wide
- 60 inches white silk or lining fabric, 45 inches wide
- Gold machine embroidery thread
- White sewing thread
- Ruler
- 2B pencil
- Sun/moon rubber stamp
- Large star rubber stamp
- Small star rubber stamp
- Fabric paint ink pad in green and purple
- Stencil cream (creme) paints in green, red, and yellow
- Turpentine or paint thinner
- Selection of brushes
- Package tape or strong masking tape
- 5 gold sun or star buttons
- Sewing machine

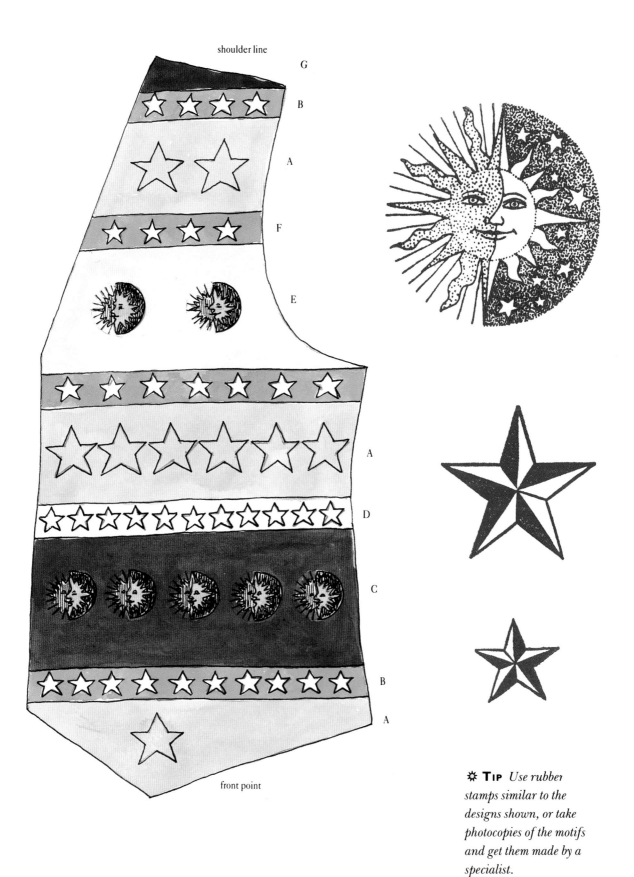

shoulder line

G

B

A

F

E

A

D

C

B

A

front point

✸ **TIP** *Use rubber stamps similar to the designs shown, or take photocopies of the motifs and get them made by a specialist.*

5 Use the small star stamp and the purple ink pad and print areas B, D, and F with the correct amount of stars.

6 Using the sun/moon stamp and the purple pad, print areas C and E with the correct amount of suns. Repeat for the other side. Leave the fabric to dry for a few hours.

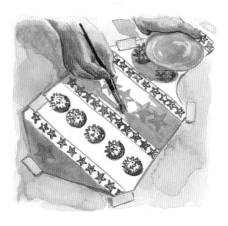

7 Fill a shallow container with a little turpentine or paint thinner and use a ½-inch brush with the yellow stencil paint. Wet the brush with turpentine, then dip it into the paint. Do not allow the paint to become too runny. Cover areas A with the paint. You should be able to paint over the stamp motif without obscuring it.

8 Use a fine brush with the yellow stencil paint and fill in the sun and the rays leaving the moon-half white in area C and E. Fill in every second star with yellow in areas D and F.

9 Clean the brushes with the turpentine, then use the red stencil paint to fill in area C; painting the area between the sun rays. Do *not* paint over the motif. Fill in area G with red.

10 Begin again with clean brushes and green paint and paint *around* the stars in areas B and F. Leave the fabric to dry overnight.

11 Set the sewing machine to zigzag stitch. Set the stitch length to very fine and the stitch width to the widest setting – about ¼ inch. Use gold thread for the top thread and the bobbin. Satin stitch along each line between the rows of patterns, covering the seams. Repeat for the other front.

12 Press the fabric with a medium hot iron to set the paint (see the manufacturer's instructions). Use a pressing cloth if required.

13 Make the vest as directed on pages 108–11.

14 To finish the vest, trim it with gold sun or star buttons

✲ **TIP** *The stencil cream paint has been recommended because of its consistency; it does not "bleed" into other colors, provided it is not thinned down too much.*

DELICATE ROSEBUDS ARE SCATTERED OVER A CREAM BACKGROUND. THE EMBROIDERY
TECHNIQUE IS CROSS-STITCH ON EVENWEAVE LINEN, AND EACH MOTIF TAKES ONLY ABOUT
AN HOUR TO COMPLETE.

ROSEBUD CROSS-STITCH VEST

✿ ✿ ✿ ✿ ✿ ✿ ✿ ✿ ✿ ✿ ✿ ✿ ✿ ✿ ✿ ✿ ✿

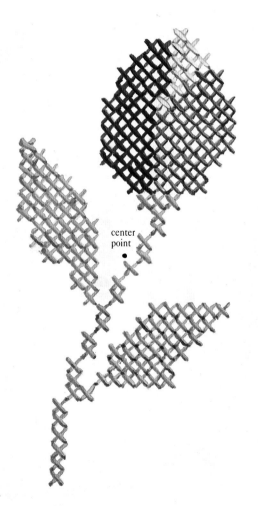

center
point

1 Trace the vest template from the patterns given on pages 118–19.

2 Lay the evenweave linen on a flat surface and pin the pattern piece in place, right side up on the right-hand side of the fabric.

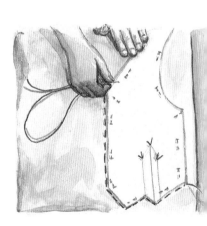

✿ **TIP** *Cross-stitch can be worked from either the left or the right, but it is important that the uppermost diagonal of all crosses should lie in the same direction.*

3 Baste around the outline and mark the darts.

MATERIALS

❁

- Basic sewing equipment
- Tapestry needle size 24
- 1 yard cream even-weave linen (28 threads per inch), 36 inches wide
- 50 inches cream lining, 45 inches wide
- Stranded floss in the following shades: 1 skein each of pale rose pink, medium rose pink, deep rose pink; 2 skeins of lime
- Embroidery hoop 8-inch diameter
- 5 × ¾-inch self-cover buttons

4 Remove the paper pattern and reverse it, then repeat the process. You will now have the vest outline on the fabric.

5 Thread the tapestry needle with three strands of the lime embroidery thread, which is best cut into 18-inch lengths.

6 To begin the first stitch, measure 2½ inches up from the peak of the right-hand vest front. This point corresponds to the center point of the colored chart of the rosebud. Work the center stitch first.

7 Do *not* tie a knot in the thread. Instead, leave a length of 1½ inches on the back which should be caught into the first few stitches on the reverse to secure it. If this is difficult, you can slip it under the back stitches later.

8 Bring the thread to the surface from the lower right-hand side and re-insert the needle two threads up and two threads to the left and bring it out two threads down. You should now have a half cross. Continue this way to the end of a row if required.

✿ **TIP** *Stranded floss usually comes in skeins of six strands. It can be used in varying thicknesses. For this project, use three strands. To create a smoother thread, it is best to separate all the strands, then recombine the number you require.*

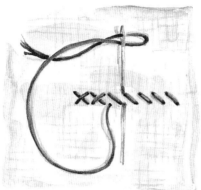

9 To complete a single stitch, bring the thread from the bottom left two threads up and two threads to the right and re-insert. This will form the top half of your cross stitch. Complete all the crosses on the row.

10 Continue to work the stem and leaves in the lime thread before working on the bud.

11 Each bud has been placed 5 inches from the center stitch and alternate motifs have been reversed. Mirror and repeat the design for the left side.

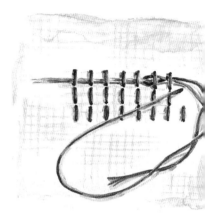

12 To fasten off the thread, run a thread under the reverse of a few stitches to secure it.

13 To complete, press lightly on the reverse and make as directed in the finishing section on pages 108–11.

14 Cover the buttons in a matching or a contrasting fabric as required and sew them on.

DEEP OCEAN-BLUE VELVET HAS BEEN DECORATED WITH STYLIZED KISSING FISH. SPIRAL EMBROIDERY ADDS AN INTERESTING TEXTURE TO THE VELVET AND IS THE BASIC MOTIF IN THIS UNUSUAL DESIGN.

ROMANTIC VELVET FISH VEST

TEMPLATES

DESIGN GUIDE

MATERIALS

☼

- Basic sewing equipment
- 1⅛ yards blue velvet, 45 inches wide
- 8 inches of green shot silk, 45 inches wide
- 8 inches of gold shot silk, 45 inches wide
- 8 inches of pink shot silk, 45 inches wide
- 1⅔ yards of black silk lining, 45 inches wide
- 20 inches fusible web
- 1⅛ yards lightweight fusible interfacing, 45 inches wide
- 5 × ¾-inch self-cover buttons
- Scissors: dressmaking and embroidery
- Embroidery thread in golden yellow, orange, turquoise, pink
- 16 inches matching blue cord
- Machine embroidery hoop, 10-inch diameter
- Sewing machine
- Iron
- 8 × 10-inch sheet of tracing paper
- Colored pencil
- 2 large sheets of tissue paper

1 Trace the pattern given for the velvet fish vest on pages 124–5. Pin it in place on top of the blue velvet and baste around the pattern, marking all edges as well as the darts. Do not use chalk as it will mark the velvet.

2 Lay the fusible web glue side down over the heart motif shown, and using a colored pencil trace six hearts, spacing them economically.

3 Trim the area with the motifs marked and iron onto the reverse of the pink fabric, glue-side down. Trim around each heart.

4 Lay the tracing paper over the fish motifs A to D and trace using the colored pencil.

5 Reverse the paper. Lay the fusible interfacing glue side down on top and trace motif A three times, spacing them economically.

6 Trim each section and iron them onto the reverse of the gold fabric. Trim around each fish.

7 Repeat motif A, tracing it onto the fusible web four times. Trim and iron them on the reverse of the green fabric (the fourth motif is worked around the dart marking). Trim around the fish.

8 Repeat for motif B – 3 × gold, 4 × green; motif C – 3 × gold, 3 × green; motif D – 3 × gold, 3 × green. You should now have 26 fish and 6 hearts trimmed and ready to be placed on the vest.

9 Enlarge the diagram (left), to full size and trace the outlines. Pin onto velvet, then baste the outline edge of the design. Mark the center points of the hearts. Pin the hearts and kissing fish in place.

10 Add in the extra dart fish and single fish. Press them into place.

11 Set the machine to do free embroidery by removing the presser foot and lowering the feed dog. Thread the machine with turquoise thread on top and pink thread in the bobbin. Loosen the bobbin tension slightly by turning the screw on the bobbin case. This will create a series of small dots of pink on top of the turquoise thread during embroidery.

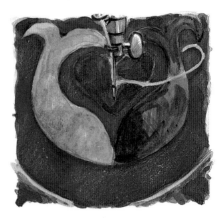

12 Position the fabric in the hoop. Place this on the machine and *lower* the presser foot bar to activate the tension. Begin to embroider around the outline of each fish slowly but smoothly, following the diagram on page 68.

13 Make a line for the fish head about ⅜ inch from the tip, then make a spiral for the eye before filling the body part with "scales." Repeat for all the fish, then outline each heart.

14 Thread the machine with orange thread on top and yellow bobbin thread. Mark with basting stitches, the areas to be given swirls. Work within the shapes you have basted and fill them with swirls. Do not outline them unless you want a more solid effect.

15 Link each fish motif with a simple wavy line embellished with two swirls. Remove basting stitches.

16 Trim each panel and assemble as directed on pages 108–11. Cut the blue cord into five even lengths and stitch one on the left side of the vest on top of the lining. Wrap each stitch over the cord loop until you have a smooth band of satin stitching. This will prevent fraying. Repeat for the other four loops. Cover five buttons in velvet embroidered with gold swirls as before and stitch them in place down the right-hand side of the vest as shown on p.68.

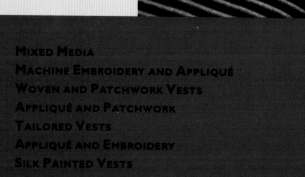

GALLERY

MIXED MEDIA

This striking collection shows what an ideal garment the vest is for demonstrating a variety of decorative techniques. Some techniques are combined to create more intricate effects; for example screen-printed fabric can be worked into patchwork designs before being embroidered.

✿   ✿   ✿   ✿   ✿   ✿   ✿   ✿   ✿   ✿   ✿   ✿   ✿   ✿   ✿

CAROLINE KEILL
(above and right)
Screen-printed velvet has been embossed using couched gold thread and machine embroidery. The back panel is made from a recycled curtain.

TORIA CHAUMETON
(top and bottom)
A vivid palette of mixed shades of crushed velvet and silk are patched in squares alongside randomly placed printed patches in coordinating colors.

CAROLINE KEILL
(above)
Screen-printed gold and black fabrics have been patched together in strips and highlighted by embroidering with metallic threads.

ROSEMARY MACCARTHY-MORROGH *(top)*
A photograph of a cluster of daisies was the inspiration for this vest, which was worked on white linen, hand-painted, embroidered, and beaded.

DEBORAH GONET
(bottom)
The traditional colors and shapes of heraldic symbols are recreated using a combination of machine embroidery and patched silk and velvet.

MACHINE EMBROIDERY AND APPLIQUÉ

Jacqueline Farrell's vests are mainly created from luxury fabrics such as linen and silk. Her favorite technique is machine embroidery over appliqué shapes, with imagery derived from natural forms and contemporary motifs.

JACQUELINE FARRELL
(above left)
Bright bluebells, rosebuds, and asters are appliquéd on dupion silk attached by free machine embroidery.

JACQUELINE FARRELL
(above center)
A bold design on linen-look silk is given a delicate touch with machine embroidery.

JACQUELINE FARRELL
(above right)
Appliquéd stars in bright colors and whimsical detail in bright green thread give a lighthearted, festive impression.

JACQUELINE FARRELL
(above left)
Rambling ivy leaves entwined
with little purple flowers are
appliquéd onto velvet, quilted
with machine embroidery.

JACQUELINE FARRELL
(above center)
Bold sunflowers appliquéd onto
silk dupion are interlaced with
machine-embroidered scrolls
and a scattering of leaves.

JACQUELINE FARRELL
(above right)
Black velvet provides a foil for
the crimson roses, creating a
winter color scheme. The detail
is machine embroidered.

WOVEN AND PATCHWORK VESTS

Handwoven fabrics can create lovely textural vests, which can either exploit the fabric texture or focus on the color. An effective way of employing color is to use one color in a variety of shades in a patchwork combination.

KATE HAYNES *(top)*
Woven stripes form a cotton and silk doublecloth fabric.
(center) The weave technique of "figuring" allows distinct images to be created at strategic points.

POOKIE BLEZARD
(right)
Earthy tones, well-balanced proportions, and interesting textures combine successfully in this patchwork vest.

GEORGINA VON ETZDORF
(center)
Gold and wine corded fabric gives this woven fabric vest a warm, rich look.

KATE HAYNES
(top center)
Minimalist color and hand-woven pleats produce a wonderfully understated vest in cool tones.

JANET GEORGE *(bottom)*
An intricately woven wool fabric in bright variegated bands and a rich red tartan are made into two vests with classic lines.

TORIA CHAUMETON
(top right)
Harlequin checked silk in heraldic colors makes a stylish vest. Note the neat collar lapels.

Appliqué and Patchwork

Patchwork is an economic and effective method of using up small pieces of fabric. To add extra detail, the patchwork fabric can be quilted or embroidered after construction.

Deborah Gonet

(bottom)

Individual squares of silks and velvets are appliquéd and embroidered with a kaleidescope of images and textures.

Judith Gait

(top right)

Crazy patchwork using silk dupion fabric in three colors is overstitched with contrasting machine embroidery in satin stitch.

Pookie Blezard

(bottom)

Two vest shapes and one technique: patchwork strips. A high stand-up collar offers an alternative to the traditional V-neck vest.

❊ ❊ ❊ ❊ ❊ ❊   ❊ ❊ ❊ ❊ ❊ ❊ ❊ ❊ ❊

DEBORAH GONET
(above left)
Huge fun sunflowers are
appliquéd onto this plain linen
vest. The edges are left raw
and deliberately frayed for a
realistic look which adds texture.

TORIA CHAUMETON
(far top left)
Coordinating strips of tapestry fabrics are stitched
together to produce a unique patchwork fabric for
this handsome vest. *(above right and center)* This
magnificent long-line vest in stained-glass patchwork
features a wonderful array of floral prints.

TAILORED VESTS

Tailored vests require more
complex techniques than the
finishing featured in this book.
However, Tom Gilbey's creative
use of sumptuous materials,
hand-painting, screen-printing,
embroidery, and other details
provides great inspiration.

✿ ✿ ✿ ✿ ✿ ✿ ✿ ✿ ✿ ✿ ✿ ✿ ✿ ✿ ✿ ✿ ✿

TOM GILBEY
(above left)
This bold heraldic imagery is
created from machine
embroidered appliqué,
decorated with sparkling jewels.

TOM GILBEY
(above center)
Black and white images of
famous people and places are
screen-printed onto white silk,
so that the overall design is
graduated from dark to light.

TOM GILBEY
(above right)
Fun metal and fabric badges
with images based on a
transportation theme customize
a purchased vest. This is a great
way of displaying souvenirs.

✻ ✻ ✻ ✻ ✻ ✻ ✻ ✻ ✻ ✻ ✻ ✻ ✻ ✻ ✻ ✻ ✻

TOM GILBEY
(above top and bottom)
This exclusive image from an auction showroom lends itself to being hand-painted on silk in subtle tones which are carried through to the back.

TOM GILBEY
(above center)
Quilted hearts interlaced with gold embroidery and three-dimensional gold roses stand out on a cream silk background.

TOM GILBEY
(above right)
A glossy black background fabric is the perfect foil for pretty floral tapestry hearts. The appliquéd hearts are interlinked with couched gold cord.

APPLIQUÉ AND EMBROIDERY

Any material can be used to decorate vests, as this collection shows. Appliquéd strips of ribbon are effective, and distorted hand knitting creates an unusual fabric texture. Both ideas and materials can be "recycled" in this way.

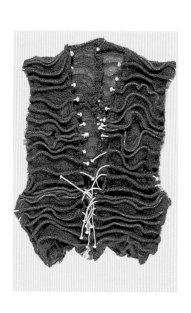

JANET AND ROGER QUILTER
(left and center)
Appliqué images, based on characters from Dylan Thomas' *Under Milkwood*, are quilted onto this pictorial vest.

JO HALL
(bottom right)
This fragile-looking vest is constructed of machine-knitted fabric threaded with string to create a unique "natural" garment.

ELSPETH KEMP
(top right)
Suede binding with an unusual line frames the embroidered panel of this crossover-style vest.

SILK PAINTED VESTS

Fabric-painted vests can be as subtle or as bold as the designer chooses. Translucent watercolor effects show up best on white silk, while opaque paints can be painted over a dark fabric.

ALISON BELL

(left)

This child's vest is decorated with animal characters from favorite stories, handpainted on silk, then highlighted with gold pen.

CATHERINE CROWTHER

(center)

Pale yellow painted silk provides a foil for the stenciled sun and moon images, which are highlighted in gold.

CATHERINE CROWTHER

(top)

A floral design in pastel shades is painted on silk using a batik wax-resist technique.

SALLY CUNNINGHAM
(above)
Randomly painted strips of silk
are patched together and woven
into an openwork construction.
Machine embroidery secures
and highlights each strip.

ALISON BELL
(left center)
These bands of color have been
painted onto silk to resemble
rock strata, creating a fantasy
landscape for a host of
humorous animal outlines.

SUSIE MOORE
(right center)
A few large images and clear
colors combine in this discreet
but amusing painted tea cup
vest.

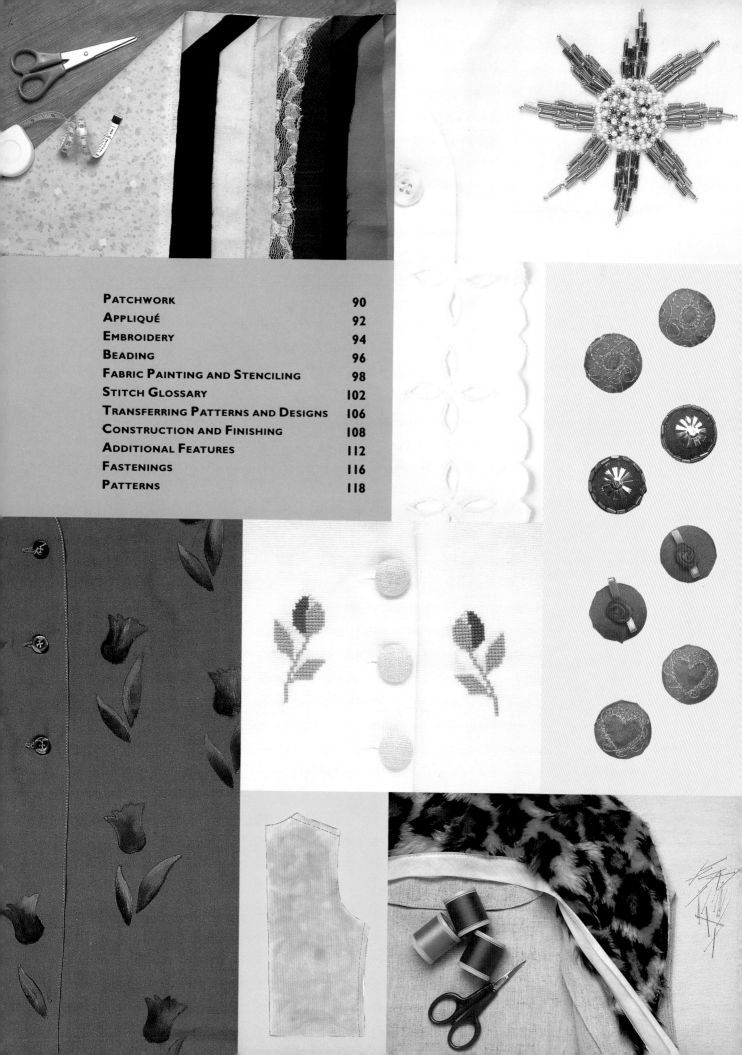

TECHNIQUES AND PATTERNS

IN PATCHWORK SMALL PIECES OF CLOTH ARE CUT INTO REGULAR SHAPES AND JOINED
TOGETHER EITHER BY HAND OR MACHINE STITCHING. THE PIECES USED CAN BE IN MATCHING
SHADES OR CONTRASTING COLORS, AND THE COMBINED EFFECT OF THE SHAPES AND COLORS
CREATES A WHOLE NEW PIECE OF FABRIC WITH AN INTRICATE DESIGN. PATCHWORK ORIGINATED
AS AN ECONOMIC WAY OF PRODUCING LARGE PIECES OF CLOTH FROM RECYCLED MATERIALS.

PATCHWORK

Some of the oldest examples of
patchwork are quilts. They have a
geometric design made up of
squares, triangles, diamonds, and
rectangles which were made by
simply folding and cutting the
fabric. Around the mid-nineteenth
century, templates were introduced
which gave rise to more elaborate
designs such as the widely used
honeycomb pattern.

Materials and equipment

Any kind of material can be used to
make patchwork, but it is easier to
work with fabrics of the same
thickness. Cotton is the most
popular as it is available in a wide
variety of colors and designs, keeps
its shape, and is easy to cut, fold, and
sew neatly. When fabrics of
different weights are sewn together,
the finer one may tear. It is also
more difficult to fold and sew heavy
fabric to an exact size, and uneven-
sized patches can distort the overall
pattern. However, crazy patchwork

takes advantage of these factors. It
can be made from a wide variety of
pieces in different colors, shapes,
weights, and textures arranged in a
random pattern. The striking effect
produced this way makes excellent
fabric for a vest.

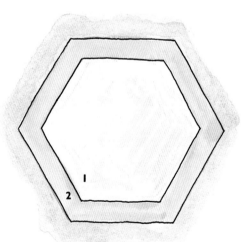

1. paper templates
2. fabric template with ¼in seam
   allowance

ENGLISH PATCHWORK

IN TRADITIONAL ENGLISH
PATCHWORK, THE FABRIC
PIECES ARE BASTED ONTO
IDENTICAL PAPER SHAPES SUCH
AS HEXAGONS OR DIAMONDS,
THEN SEWN TOGETHER TO
CREATE A PATTERN.

1 Cut templates 1 and 2 from thin
cardboard using a craft knife
and cutting board. Cut plenty of
paper shapes from clean paper
using template 1.

2 To make sure the paper shapes
are identical, cut them on a
board using a craft knife pressed
against the side of the template. Do

not draw around a template and then cut it out as the result will not be accurate. Using template 2, trace fabric shapes on different pieces of material until you think you have enough to make your article. Cut them out accurately with scissors. Check the quantity against the garment pattern by laying the fabric shapes on top. You can plan the arrangement of the colors and figure out the pattern at this stage.

3 Baste a paper shape onto the back of each fabric shape, turning the raw edges to the back and basting them down as you go.

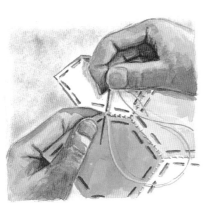

4 Hold the backed fabric shapes face to face and stitch along one side, overcasting with close firm stitches.

Continue sewing the shapes together, building up the pattern in this manner until the patchwork is the size needed for the article you wish to make. You can now use the patchwork like an ordinary piece of fabric. When you have finished sewing the article, remove all basting stitches and take out the paper.

AMERICAN PATCHWORK

AMERICAN PATCHWORK QUILTS WERE OFTEN PIECED TOGETHER FROM SQUARE BLOCKS. THE BLOCKS WERE EASILY PORTABLE AND COULD BE STORED UNTIL THERE WERE ENOUGH TO MAKE THE FINISHED ARTICLE. MANY QUILTS WERE MADE COMMUNALLY IN THIS WAY. QUICK METHODS FOR ASSEMBLING THE BLOCKS WERE DEVISED, AND BLOCK PATCHWORK CAN ALSO BE DONE EASILY ON A SEWING MACHINE.

1 Draw a block pattern using graph paper. Divide the block into equal squares. Further divide the alternate blocks into two triangles. You will need only two templates: 1 – the full square and 2 – the triangle. Transfer the shapes from your block diagram onto cardboard and cut them out.

2 Choose three contrasting or, if you prefer, coordinated fabrics and cut the required shapes, adding a ¼ inch seam allowance all around each shape.

3 Machine stitch the triangles together to form a square, then stitch each square together to make one block using the ¼ inch seam allowance.

Alternate the colors in each block, then machine-stitch all the blocks together until you have enough fabric to make two symmetrical vest fronts.

4 Press all seams open and trim excess bulk wherever several seams meet. Press seams between light and dark colors toward the dark fabric, as they may show through the light fabric.

✿ **TIP** *Remember a smaller block is best for a small garment like a vest, as it has to be repeated over a fairly small area.*

APPLIQUÉ IS THE TECHNIQUE OF STITCHING CUTOUT SHAPES ONTO A FINISHED BACKGROUND TO CREATE A RAISED, DECORATIVE MOTIF ON CLOTHING OR FURNISHINGS. APPLIQUÉ MOTIFS CAN BE STITCHED ON BY HAND USING PLAIN SEWING OR AN EMBROIDERY STITCH, WHICH GIVES A DECORATIVE EDGING. OR THEY MAY BE SEWN ON BY MACHINE, AND THIS OPERATION CAN BE COMBINED WITH MACHINE EMBROIDERY, TOO.

APPLIQUÉ

❀ ❀ ❀ ❀ ❀ ❀ ❀ ❀ ❀ ❀ ❀ ❀ ❀ ❀ ❀ ❀

Originally, appliqué was a functional technique – for sewing patches on knees and elbows, or attaching badges or labels. But now it is used extensively for decorating garments, quilts, throw pillows, and other objects.

There are various types of appliqué, including reverse appliqué, known as mola work. Bold, simple designs can be stitched straight on. For more complex ones involving very small motifs, fusible web is usually used. Shapes can be interfaced first to give them more body or to stop the fabric from fraying too much. Fusible web also allows shapes to be trimmed very

precisely and then heat-pressed in position before being stitched. Small pieces of fabric, stitched on and then deliberately frayed, exploit the texture of a raw edge.

Appliqué can also be quilted, or decorated further with different embroidery stitches such as buttonhole stitch. For a very elaborate effect, beads, sequins, feathers, and other objects can be sewn onto the appliqué motif. It also provides the ideal means for attaching initials to personalize a garment.

TURNED-EDGE APPLIQUÉ

THIS IS THE MOST COMMON METHOD OF APPLIQUÉ, WHICH HAS LONG BEEN USED ON QUILTS, GARMENTS, FABRICS WHICH FRAY, AND FOR PADDED MOTIFS.

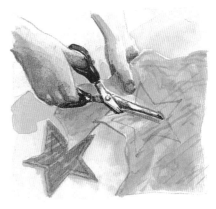

1 Cut out each pattern piece including a seam allowance of ¼–½ inch.

2 Baste or bond interfacing on the reverse to fit the finished size of each piece.

3 Turn the seam allowance under on the reverse side and baste it down. Prepare all the appliqué shapes like this.

4 Stretch the required area of the background fabric over an embroidery frame and pin and baste each appliqué shape in place, working from the background to foreground if they are superimposed.

5 Slipstitch along the edge of each shape with tiny stitches close to the edge of the motif. Remove the basting stitches. Avoid pressing an appliqué motif as ironing tends to flatten it and spoil the effect.

MACHINE APPLIQUÉ

MACHINE APPLIQUÉ IS QUICK, AND ADDED TEXTURE CAN BE PROVIDED BY COMBINING THE APPLIQUÉ WITH MACHINE EMBROIDERY.

1 Iron a sheet of fusible web onto the reverse of appliqué fabric. Trace and then cut out the motifs, peel off the backing sheet, and use an iron to bond the motifs to the background fabric.

2 Machine-stitch around the motif outline. Use satin stitch or another automatic machine stitch. For a free effect, you can attach the motifs with machine embroidery lines and scrolls. The bonding will help prevent fraying.

PERSIAN APPLIQUÉ

THIS NINETEENTH-CENTURY TECHNIQUE IMITATES DETAILED EMBROIDERY BY ATTACHING TRIMMED PRINTED MOTIFS TO A BACKGROUND FABRIC.

1 Cut out the printed motifs and bond them in place.

2 Secure the motifs with satin stitch by hand or machine or by using another hand embroidery stitch, stab stitching, or overcast stitching.

DECORATIVE EDGES

DECORATIVE STITCHES CAN ALSO BE USED TO FINISH THE EDGES ON EITHER TURNED-EDGE OR RAW-EDGE APPLIQUÉ.

1 Suitable stitches are cretan stitch, feather stitch, and buttonhole stitch (see Stitch Glossary, pages 102–5). These stitches should enhance the design, but are not intended to form the focal point.

EMBROIDERY CAN ADD EXTRA ORNAMENT TO ANY SEWING PROJECT, WHETHER IT STARTS OUT AS PLAIN OR PAINTED FABRIC, PATCHWORK, OR APPLIQUÉ. HAND EMBROIDERING A LARGE PIECE OF FABRIC, SUCH AS A GARMENT, TAKES A LONG TIME, BUT WITH A MODERN SEWING MACHINE, BEAUTIFUL DESIGNS CAN BE COMPLETED VERY QUICKLY. IF YOU DO NOT HAVE A SUITABLE MACHINE, ALL THE HAND EMBROIDERY STITCHES, AS WELL AS THOSE FOR PLAIN SEWING, ARE ILLUSTRATED IN THE STITCH GLOSSARY.

EMBROIDERY

✿　　✿　　✿　　✿　　✿　　✿　　✿　　✿　　✿　　✿　　✿　　✿　　✿　　✿　　✿　　✿

For machine embroidery you need an electric sewing machine with a removable spool case, so that you can adjust the tension when using thick embroidery thread, and a "feed dog" that can either be lowered or covered with a plate. You will also need a selection of machine needles in various sizes (the thicker the thread and fabric, the bigger the needle required) and an embroidery hoop to hold the fabric taut.

It takes time to get used to manipulating the fabric and controlling the speed for embroidery so always practice on a scrap of fabric first.

Experiment with the tension setting when practicing each type of stitch. The presser-foot bar must always be lowered to activate the tension, even when the presser foot itself is removed, as in freestyle embroidery.

USING A HOOP

UNLESS YOU ARE VERY EXPERIENCED, ALWAYS USE AN EMBROIDERY HOOP FOR MACHINE EMBROIDERY, WHICH IS IDEAL FOR SMALLER PIECES OF WORK.

1 Before you begin, bind the inner ring with strips of cotton binding tape. This will protect the delicate embroidery stitching as you work across the fabric areas.

2 Lay the outer ring down, place the fabric on top, face down, and insert inner ring. Tighten the fabric and screw up the outer ring. The inner ring should stand *slightly* below the outer ring to allow the fabric to contact the machine bed.

USING THE PRESSER FOOT

SOME MACHINES ARE EQUIPPED WITH A TRANSPARENT PRESSER FOOT SO THAT THE STITCHING CAN BE SEEN MORE CLEARLY.

1 Thread the machine as normal and begin straight stitching back and forth. Use different thread and stitch lengths to create texture. Build up rows of vertical and horizontal lines to create solid color.

2 Adjust the stitch width to achieve a zigzag stitch and the stitch length to achieve satin stitch. Experiment by widening and narrowing the width to create dots, blocks, and triangles in satin stitch.

✿ **TIP** *Use twin needles to sew parallel lines in similar or contrasting threads to create textural lines.*

BASTING FOOT

1 Surface loops are created using the basting foot and by adjusting the stitch width. These are good for landscape effects and textural areas.

FREE EMBROIDERY

ALWAYS USE A HOOP FOR THIS, THE MOST CREATIVE WAY OF STITCHING.

1 For free machine work, you must disengage the feed dog, reduce the stitch width to zero, and remove the presser foot.

2 Slide in the fabric in the hoop and *lower* the presser foot bar. Turn the wheel to insert the needle, then raise it and pull the bobbin thread through. Pull the thread to the left side and insert the needle again before pressing the motor drive slowly.

3 Move the frame around gently to create an area of stitching. Practice "doodling" and writing names before progressing to motifs and all-over patterns and textures.

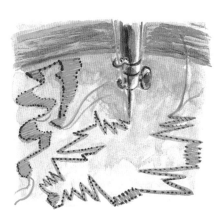

4 Adjust the stitch width to produce a free zigzag stitch. Move the hoop slowly for satin stitch, faster for zigzag wavy lines.
  Whipstitch and cable stitch can also be done by machine.

BEADS CAN BE USED TO CREATE A RICH, TEXTURED DECORATION ON GARMENTS. IN THIS CENTURY, BEADING WAS USED MOST DRAMATICALLY ON 1920'S "FLAPPER" DRESSES WHERE DENSE ROWS OF GLASS BEADS CAUGHT AND REFLECTED THE ELECTRIC LIGHT WHICH WAS NEW AT THAT TIME. IN VICTORIAN ENGLAND, BLACK JET BEADS WERE USED AS SOBER BUT LUSTROUS DECORATION ON MOURNING WEAR, A FASHION LED BY QUEEN VICTORIA AFTER THE DEATH OF PRINCE ALBERT.

BEADING

A good selection of beads can now be found in most craft stores. There are many types including rocailles, artificial seed pearls, tiny tube-shaped bugle beads, floral hand-painted ceramic beads, sequins, and many others.

Materials and equipment

Sewing on fine beads usually requires special beading needles, which are very long and fine. They are fragile and tend to bend, so you may have to replace them frequently. A strong thread is also needed – use cotton or polyester. The thread should be strengthened further by pulling it through a beeswax block. This will also prevent the thread from twisting.

Any fabric can be beaded, although lightweight fabrics may need extra backing. An embroidery hoop can be used to hold the fabric taut when beading.

EMBROIDERING WITH INDIVIDUAL BEADS

ALTHOUGH IT IS TIME-CONSUMING TO SEW ON BEADS INDIVIDUALLY, THE END RESULT IS CERTAINLY WORTHWHILE AND COULD TURN AN ORDINARY GARMENT INTO AN HEIRLOOM.

1 For fine beads you will need a fine beading needle and invisible thread or a color to match the background fabric. Knot the end of the thread and insert the needle into the right side of the fabric. Make two to three stitches on the wrong side to secure the thread firmly and bring the needle out again beside the knot.

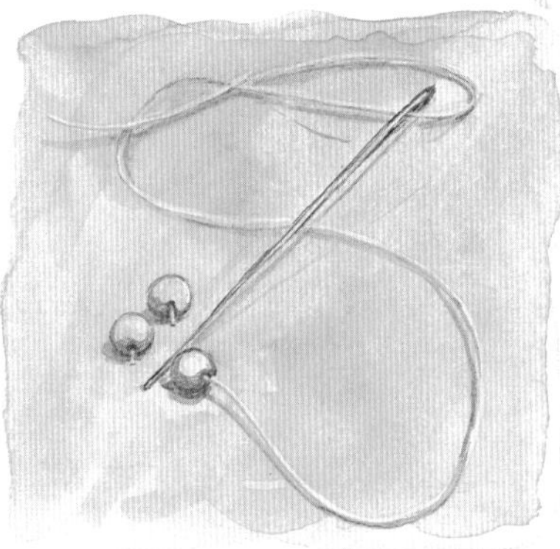

2 Thread the bead and reinsert the needle close to the point where it emerged.

3 Bring the needle up in the right position for the center of the next bead, thread the bead, reinsert the needle, and continue. Make a backstitch every third bead to secure the arrangement.

BUGLE BEADS

**BUGLE BEADS ARE TINY, TUBE-
SHAPED BEADS THAT CAN BE
LAID END TO END TO CREATE A
LUSTROUS, FLEXIBLE "PIPE" OR
CORDED EFFECT. THEY CAN
ALSO BE USED TO MAKE TINY
STAR-SHAPED FLOWERS OR
SUNBURST DESIGNS.**

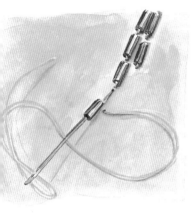

1 Sew on bugle beads in the same
way as individual beads, but
always make a backstitch through
each bead to secure it firmly.

✿ **TIP** *For theatrical costumes,
dense beading can be produced
quickly by using strong fabric glue.
You could also use this method for a
garment that will not be washed or
subjected to much wear and tear.*

COUCHING

**IT IS EASIER TO WORK OUT A
DESIGN WHEN YOU HAVE A
GROUP OF BEADS ALREADY
THREADED TOGETHER.
COUCHING SAVES TIME
BECAUSE IT IS QUICKER TO
THREAD SEVERAL BEADS AT
ONE TIME, THAN INDIVIDUAL
BEADS AT INTERVALS.**

1 Knot the end of the thread,
bring it through to the surface
of the fabric, and thread on the
beads.

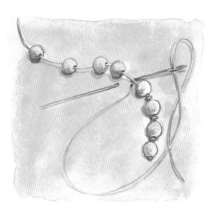

2 Use a *separate* needle and thread
to make a small overcast stitch
across the bead thread as close as
possible to the first bead. Slide each
bead up in turn and secure with the
couching thread. When finished,
secure the couching thread on the
reverse, then the beaded thread.

✿ **TIP** *You can use a
decorative thread and
French knots in between
beads for added color.
(See French Knots
pages 102–5.)*

ATTACHING FRINGING

**BEADED FRINGES MAKE A
DRAMATIC AND DECORATIVE
EDGE TO EVENING WEAR.**

1 Decide on the finished length of
the fringe and cut the thread to
twice the length plus a 4-inch
allowance for sewing and knotting
the thread.

2 Thread the beads by taking a
single thread through the
bottom bead, then the double
thread through the remainder of
the beads. Stitch the loose ends
through the fabric and finish by
knotting ends together.

3 Alternatively, knot the thread
and bring the needle through to
the right side of the fabric, thread
on enough beads to make the
complete bead loop, then reinsert
the needle next to the point where it
emerged. Overcast the ends a few
times and finish off on the reverse.

HAND PAINTING ON FABRIC IS AN ANCIENT CRAFT FIRST PRACTICED ON NATURAL SILK IN THE

FAR EAST. THE SHEEN OF FINE SILK COMBINES WITH THE TRANSLUCENT COLORS OF FABRIC

PAINTS TO CREATE A BEAUTIFUL EFFECT. MODERN FABRIC PAINTS WITH SPECIAL APPLICATORS

CAN BE USED TO CREATE A WIDE VARIETY OF FINISHES, RANGING FROM A METALLIC LOOK TO

THREE-DIMENSIONAL RAISED EFFECTS AND BEADING. FABRIC PAINTS ARE OFTEN USED IN

CONJUNCTION WITH STENCILS.

FABRIC PAINTING AND STENCILING

✵ ✵ ✵ ✵ ✵ ✵ ✵ ✵ ✵ ✵ ✵ ✵ ✵ ✵ ✵ ✵

Whereas Chinese silk painting has remained an unbroken tradition, in Europe the popularity of painted fabric was replaced by the demand for printed fabric as printing techniques developed. Fabric painting is now enjoying a revival, particularly among craft workers, and colorfast fabric dyes which can be fixed with a hot iron are widely available.

In addition to silk, some synthetic fabrics, cotton, and linen can be

used for fabric painting, provided the correct type of fabric paint is used.

The paints can be applied in a wide variety of ways using brushes, sponges, pens, sprays, stamp shapes, squeegee, and rollerball nozzles. Resist techniques allow areas of color to be applied without the colors running together or bleeding. Other methods, such as the salt technique, take advantage of the effects produced by colors mixing and flowing together.

Designs can be done freestyle, but several techniques involve the use of stencils to apply different colors to particular areas of the design. Stencils are particularly useful for producing repeat patterns.

Fabric painting

All fabric painting techniques require similar basic equipment:

- Wash and dry fabric before painting to allow for shrinkage and color fading.
- It is best to use a stretcher frame to hold the fabric taut.
- Use a variety of brushes of different thicknesses for applying color washes or fine detail.
- A thinner is needed for oil-based paints, or a jar of clean water for water-based paints.
- Rags should be used to clean and dry brushes between colors.
- Practice the technique on scraps of the fabric.
- Collect examples and sketches of design ideas to copy, trace, or develop from your imagination.
- To "fix" the colors and finish of painted fabric, either press with a hot iron or steam as directed by the paint manufacturer's directions.

PAINTING ON SILK: RESIST METHOD

THIS ALLOWS DETAILED AREAS TO BE DRAWN AND STRONG AREAS OF COLOR TO BE PLACED NEXT TO EACH OTHER WITHOUT "BLEEDING."

1 Stretch the fabric across the frame and pin in place. Sketch the design lightly onto the silk with a soluble fabric marker pen, or place a drawing directly underneath.

3 Fill in the areas with liquid silk paint. Begin in the middle of a shape and work nearly to the gutta outline. The paint will spread by itself. You can build the color gradually to a strong intensity, leaving it to dry between "coats."

1 Brush the fabric with water (or thinner if using oil-based paints) according to the manufacturer's directions, then quickly apply the paints onto the wet silk. Start with lighter tones working up or down a panel to darker tones. Add detail by painting in shapes such as trees on a landscape background. Add more fine detail as the work begins to dry as the colors will not flow as much.

2 Brush on water (or thinner) to break up areas that appear too solid. Dark watermark edges will appear, but these can be considered part of the final design.

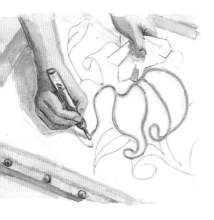

PAINTING ON SILK: WATER-COLOR METHOD

2 Trace over the outlines on the silk using a gutta pen (clear, gold, or silver) and leave to dry. Clean the nozzle with a tissue frequently to stop blobs from forming. The gutta acts as barrier between the areas of color.

THIS TECHNIQUE DOES NOT USE OUTLINER. INSTEAD, THE COLORS ARE ENCOURAGED TO FLOW INTO ONE ANOTHER. THE TECHNIQUE CAN ALSO BE ADAPTED FOR USE WITH OIL-BASED PAINTS, USING A THINNER TO MAKE THE COLORS FLOW.

PAINTING ON SILK: SALT METHOD

THIS TECHNIQUE CAN BE USED TO PRODUCE A STRIKING EFFECT ON ITS OWN, OR IT CAN BE COMBINED WITH EITHER THE RESIST OR WATERCOLOR TECHNIQUES.

1 Scatter salt over damp, freshly painted areas of the fabric. The salt absorbs the water and pigment, so a marbled and clouded effect results. Leave the salt and silk to dry before brushing the salt off.

Table salt and coarse sea salt produce different effects. To make it more effective, dry the salt in a warm oven before use.

EMBOSSED FABRIC PAINTS

EMBOSSED FABRIC PAINTS CAN BE USED ON THEIR OWN FOR A CORDED OR BEADED EFFECT, OR ON TOP OF ALREADY PAINTED FABRIC TO CREATE A RAISED 3-D EFFECT. THESE PAINTS COME IN A SQUEEZE TUBE WITH A SPECIAL NOZZLE.

1 Squeeze the tube gently but firmly and draw either smooth flowing lines or a series of dots. Colors can be placed next to each other as they should not run. Leave to dry overnight.

CREME PAINTS

CREME (CREAM) FABRIC PAINT USUALLY COMES IN SMALL JARS AND IS OIL-BASED SO YOU WILL ALSO NEED THINNER.

1 Mark the design outline onto the fabric using a soluble fabric marker pen. Pour the thinner into a shallow container, and using the creme paint begin with the light areas within a shape, then the darker tones. Blend the tones as you go, thinning the paint colors as required. When the paint is touch-dry, add highlights and details.

STENCILING

STENCILING IS ASSOCIATED MAINLY WITH DECORATIVE WALL BORDERS, BUT MANY TEXTILE DESIGNERS ALSO USE STENCILS. IN THIS TECHNIQUE THE DRAWINGS ARE STYLIZED, A COMMON FEATURE OF FOLK ART, AND THIS MAKES REPEAT DESIGNS EASY.

THE BASIC TOOLS REQUIRED ARE A SELECTION OF STENCIL PAINTS (NOT CRAYONS), STENCIL BRUSHES IN A FEW SIZES, SOME PAPER TOWELS, AN ERASER, MASKING TAPE, AND A PRE-CUT STENCIL DESIGN ON CARDBOARD OR ACETATE FILM.

colored areas of the design if it is very detailed. Alternatively, you can mask off the unwanted "holes."

Make a central registration mark on your design that won't be cut out and mark this point on each stencil sheet so that you can overlay exactly each time.

2 Tape the stencil to the fabric. Dip your brush into the first color, and remove excess paint. Brush to the outline of the stencil shape with a circular motion, keeping the brush vertical. With large cut-out areas you can add shading and highlights. Allow the first color to dry and clean the stencil before applying the second color. Mask off unwanted areas, or use separate stencils for designs which combine different colors.

1 To make your own stencil design, lay a sheet of thick acetate over a sketch of your design and trace the outlines, keeping it as simple as possible. Lay the acetate on the cutting mat and cut out the shapes cleanly with a craft knife. Leave narrow "bridges" connecting the inner parts of the design to the edge of the outline. You can make separate stencils for different

3 Leave the fabric to dry for 24 hours before heat-setting it with a cool iron and a dry pressing cloth or as directed by the paint manufacturer.

THERE ARE MANY TYPES OF HAND-EMBROIDERY STITCHES. SOME, SUCH AS LAZY-DAISY STITCH, ARE MAINLY DECORATIVE, WHILE SOME PERFORM A FUNCTION AS WELL, SUCH AS HERRINGBONE, WHICH CAN BE USED TO OVERCAST A HEM.

STITCH GLOSSARY

Freestyle embroidery

Freestyle embroidery can be done on almost any fabric with any thread; and by experimenting with weights of fabric and thread combinations, you can produce wonderful patterns and textures.

Needles

You will need a variety of embroidery needles in various sizes to allow for the different types of thread and fabric, but for a novice, 2/3 strands of stranded floss and a No. 6 or 7 crewel embroidery needle are the easiest to handle.

Use an embroidery hoop for large pieces of work. To prevent the hoop from snagging fabric or the embroidery, bind the inner ring with strips of cotton tape first.

RUNNING STITCH

A simple in-and-out stitch normally used to make gathers.

BASTING STITCH

A long-and-short running stitch used to hold pieces of fabric together temporarily before machining or fine sewing.

OVERCASTING

This stitch is used to finish edges, particularly if there is a danger of the material fraying. Work from either direction, taking the thread over the edge of the fabric. Do not pull the thread too tightly.

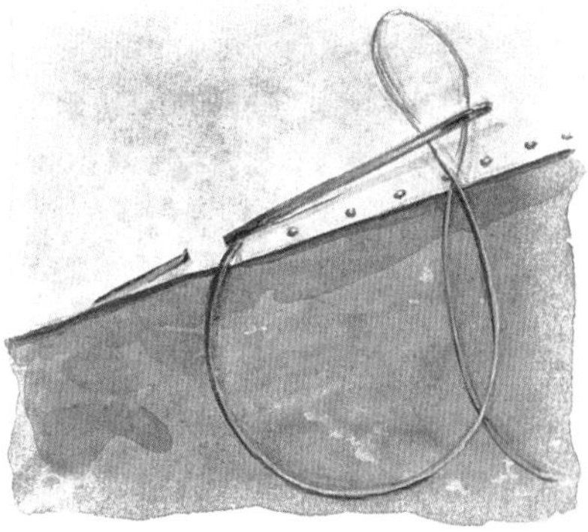

STAB STITCH

Bring the needle through to the right side. Stab the needle through the material to form a tiny stitch. Also known as prick stitch, it should be almost invisible on the right side.

SLIPSTITCH

Bring the needle through to the right side. Insert it and then bring it back up to form a neat line of small stitches.

BACKSTITCH

Bring the thread through on the stitch line, then take a small backward stitch through the fabric. Bring the needle through again a little in front of the first stitch; take another backward stitch to fill in the gap. Keep the stitches small and even. This is also known as Running Backstitch. It is good for outlining and adding detail. It can also be used for handsewing seams.

STEM STITCH

Work from left to right (if you are right-handed), taking small, regular backstitches that overlap slightly as you stitch along the line of the design. The thread should always emerge on the same side of the previous stitch so that all the overlaps lie in the same direction.

Stem stitch is used for flower stems and outlines. It can also be used as a filling stitch by working rows of stem stitch close together within a shape.

WHIPPING STITCH

By weaving or "whipping" a second, contrasting, thread through a running stitch, a very attractive plaited effect can be created.

This can be done very effectively by machine. Use a fine embroidery thread in the bobbin and a firm cotton sewing thread on top. Tighten the top tension and slightly slacken the bottom tension. Stitch quickly but move the hoop slowly. The bobbin thread will cord and cover the top thread. This is most effective with contrasting colors and can be used as a decorative top stitch on existing garments.

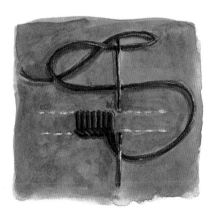

BUTTONHOLE STITCH

Bring the thread out on the lower line, insert the needle in position on the upper line, taking a straight downward stitch with the thread looped under the needle point. Pull the thread through to tighten the loop and repeat, keeping the stitches very close together. The rolled edge created by the linked loops becomes the edge of the buttonhole. Always cut the buttonhole slit *after* completing the buttonhole stitching.

Most machines will make a very good buttonhole stitch with professional-looking results.

A purely decorative version can be created by spacing the stitches more widely as in *Blanket Stitch*. It can be worked around an appliqué shape and is also used in cutwork, where the looped edge defines the area of fabric to be cut away.

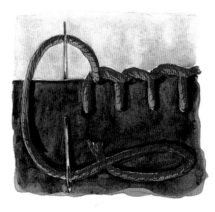

BLANKET STITCH

Work this like buttonhole stitch with the stitches spaced out.

It was traditionally used for edging woolen cloth or blankets and gives an attractive "folk" image to garments. This is also known as Detached Buttonhole Stitch.

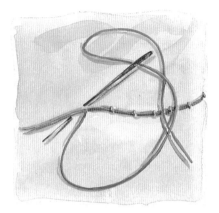

COUCHING

To "couch" a thread, lay it along the line of a design, and with another thread, anchor it down at regular intervals with small stitches through the fabric. The anchoring stitch can be self-colored and therefore invisible, or a contrasting color to the laid thread if desired. Varied weights of thread can create an interesting effect.

Couching is used for attaching cord, braid, and strings of beads.

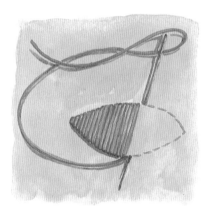

SATIN STITCH

Make rows of adjacent straight stitches, working them closely together across the shape. In a small area, such as a tiny leaf or petal, the stitches can go from edge to edge of the outline. To fill in large areas with satin stitch, make stitches of

different lengths on the first row, then fill in with more for the second row. This disguises the "seams" and gives the whole area a satin finish. On its own, this is known as Long-and-Short Stitch.

On a machine, satin stitch is done using a zigzag stitch set to almost zero stitch length.

Satin stitch is the most solid filling stitch. The shape can be padded to give a raised effect by first putting some running stitches (small evenly spaced stitches) across the area at right angles to the satin stitches. Care must be taken to keep the edges even.

CABLE STITCH

Cable stitch is a variation of chain stitch (right). It is worked in a similar way to ordinary chain stitch but in this case the thread is twisted around the needle after each chain loop, and before it enters the fabric. This makes an intervening link between the chains. The stitch follows curved lines well and makes a good filling stitch when worked solidly.

LAZY DAISY STITCH

Start by making a loop in the same way as for chain stitch, but fasten down the top of each loop with a tiny anchoring stitch over the tip. Begin the next loop alongside.

This stitch can be worked singly or in groups to form flower petals, hence the name daisy. Vary the size of the petals for a realistic effect.

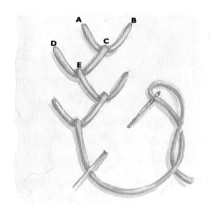

FEATHER STITCH

Bring the needle out at the center top, hold the thread down with the left thumb, insert the needle a little to the right at B on the same level, and bring the point up at C below and between A and B, keeping the thread under the needle point. Next, insert the needle at D and bring it up at E, looping the thread under the point. Then in at F and up at G, imitating the stitch at B and C. Work these two movements alternately to create the two sides of the "feather."

This stitch makes a delicate border and is very useful in floral designs.

HERRINGBONE STITCH

Bring the needle out on the lower line at the left side and insert on the upper line a little to the right. Make a small stitch to the left, keeping the thread *below* the needle. Insert the needle on the lower line a little to the right and take a small stitch to the left with the thread *above* the needle. Repeat this sequence along the line, keeping the spacing even.

Herringbone is useful as a decorative stitch or for catching and finishing a hem or raw edge.

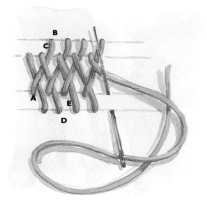

CRETAN STITCH

This is worked in a similar way to herringbone stitch and forms a zig-zag line.

Bring the thread through from the back of the fabric at A, then insert the needle vertically downward, in at B and up at C, keeping the thread under the needle. Next, the needle goes in at D, below, and up at E, vertically above D. Proceed along the line, spacing the stitches closely for Closed Cretan Stitch, or apart for Open Cretan Stitch.

It can also be worked freely to create textured effects like grass, and closed up to produce a central plait. This is a useful filling stitch.

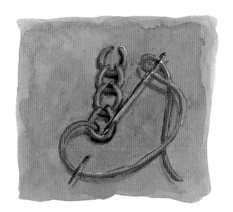

CHAIN STITCH

Starting with a knot on the end of the thread, insert the needle from

the back of the fabric, bring the thread through, and hold the working thread down with the left thumb. Reinsert the needle very close to the place where it emerged and bring the point out a short distance along the line or curve so that the working thread loops under the needle point. Pull the thread through gently. Again, insert the needle at the place it last emerged

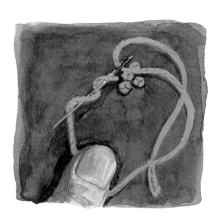

FRENCH KNOTS

Bring the thread out at the required position, hold the thread down with the left thumb, and encircle the thread twice with the needle. Still keeping the looped thread taut, twist the needle back to the starting point and insert it close to the point where it first emerged. Pull the thread through to the back and overstitch to secure a single French Knot, or work several in succession.

French Knots are useful for tiny flower centers and can be used as a filling stitch.

THERE ARE MANY WAYS OF TRANSFERRING DESIGNS TO FABRIC: FREEHAND DRAWING WITH CHALK; TRACING PAPER AND PENCIL, WHICH CAN BE ERASED ON STRONG FABRICS; DRESS-MAKER'S CARBON COPYING PAPER; BASTING AROUND THE OUTLINE; DRAWING AROUND TEM-PLATES OR STENCILS; STAMPING; PRICKING AND POUNCING; IRON-ON TRANSFERS. THE METHOD CHOSEN DEPENDS ON THE TYPES OF FABRIC BEING USED, THE DESIGN, AND THE DECORATION: THREAD, BEADS, PAINT, APPLIQUÉD FABRIC, AND SO ON.

TRANSFERRING PATTERNS AND DESIGNS

Some of the transfer methods have disadvantages when used for particular fabrics or designs.

Chalk lines wear off quickly if rubbed. They are useful as guide lines for machine embroidery, but not ideal for hand embroidery.

Dressmaker's carbon paper is a semi-permanent marker, so be sure the design positioning is correct before using it. Do not use it for fabric painting as you will be unable to cover up the lines.

More complex designs are unsuitable for tracing out by *basting* because it would become more time-consuming than the project itself.

The traditional method of *enlarging* or *reducing* a design is to use squared graph paper. This can also be done on a good photocopying machine.

TRACING THROUGH THIN FABRIC
When using a transparent or light colored fabric, it is often possible to trace the pattern directly. Lay the fabric on top of the pattern and trace it using either pencil, soluble ink, fading ink, or tailor's chalk. Move the fabric along and repeat if necessary.

DRESSMAKER'S CARBON PAPER
Dressmaker's carbon paper is similar to typing carbon paper. It is available in several colors suitable for showing up clearly on light or dark fabrics. Lay the paper face down on the right side of your fabric and place the pattern on top. Trace the lines using a dressmaker's tracing wheel.

LIGHTBOX OR WINDOW TRACING
This method allows you to trace directly onto darker fabric. Use masking tape to anchor the pattern to the lightbox or a window with bright daylight coming through. Tape the fabric on top, right side up, to keep it taut and in place. Trace the pattern using either pencil, soluble ink, fading ink, or tailor's chalk.

TRACING AROUND TEMPLATES

You can buy ready-made templates for some designs, or make your own. Cut out the template in cardboard and lay it on the fabric. Trace using pencil, soluble ink, fading ink, or tailor's chalk.

IRON-ON TRANSFERS

You can buy ready-made iron-on transfers or design your own using a transfer pencil and tracing paper. Draw or trace the design onto the tracing paper in ordinary pencil. Go over the design with a transfer pencil on the reverse. Place the transfer face down on the right side of the fabric, then press with a warm iron.

PRICKING AND POUNCING

Trace the design onto tracing paper and turn it to the reverse. Use a medium needle to prick holes close together along the design lines. Turn the paper the correct way up and place on fabric. Rub crushed dressmaker's chalk over the lines of holes using cotton balls. This leaves a fine dotted line of chalk which is easily brushed away later.

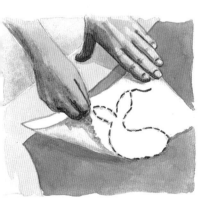

TRACING AND BASTING

Trace the design onto tissue paper and pin it to the fabric. Baste around the design. Tear away the tissue paper carefully to leave the stitched outline. If the basting is not covered by the design, remove it on completion of the work.

ENLARGING OR REDUCING A DESIGN

THERE ARE TWO BASIC METHODS FOR ENLARGING OR REDUCING DESIGNS. BOTH ARE EASY, BUT GRIDS ARE MORE TIME-CONSUMING.

PHOTOCOPYING

With a good photocopying machine, you can not only copy the chosen pattern or motif, but also enlarge or reduce it to the required size for your project.

GRIDS

1 To enlarge a sketched design of your own, carefully draw a grid of equal squares over the original pattern.

2 Draw a second grid on another sheet of paper using the same number of squares, either larger or smaller than the original ones, depending on whether you need to enlarge or reduce the design.

3 Copy the main lines of the first design onto the second grid. The squares make it easy to position the lines. Use this method to scale up the vest patterns given.

THE PROJECTS IN THIS BOOK INCLUDE BOTH ENTIRELY NEW, HOMEMADE VESTS AND TECH-NIQUES FOR DECORATING EXISTING VESTS BOUGHT NEW OR RESCUED FROM THE REJECT PILE. THE FINISHING TECHNIQUES GIVEN HERE SHOW HOW TO CONSTRUCT A BASIC VEST, WHICH CAN BE USED FOR ANY OF THE PROJECTS, WITH INSTRUCTIONS ON HOW TO ADAPT THE METHOD FOR PARTICULAR DESIGNS AND FABRICS, AS WELL AS GUIDANCE ON ALTERING PATTERN SIZES.

CONSTRUCTION AND FINISHING

✿   ✿   ✿   ✿   ✿   ✿   ✿   ✿   ✿   ✿   ✿   ✿   ✿   ✿   ✿   ✿

The following instructions describe how to make your own vest from new fabric. Beginning with figuring out your correct size, the book shows how to make a pattern, cut out the fabric, line and interface economically, and sew up the garment, fitting and altering it if necessary as you go.

Refer to the individual projects for special treatment. For example, the Summer Vest and the Mexican Felt Vest are unlined and have individual decorated edges. The position of darts and pockets must be considered in conjunction with the design, particularly in the Cherub Wedding Vest. And of course you could make your own vest to use with any of the "customizing" projects.

Ideal vests for customizing in your own style and colors can often be found by bargain hunters in secondhand clothing stores and at sales. Vests from men's suits are worth looking out for. Better still are the handsome garments bought to wear on formal occasions. Well-made and of fine fabric, they have usually had very little wear and deserve to be given a new lease on life. A few simple alterations adapted from the pattern-fitting section of the instructions will turn a hand-me-down into a snug fit.

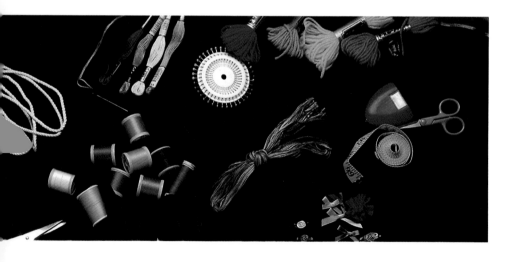

✿ **TIP** *Male buttonholes: left side of wearer. Female buttonholes: right side of wearer.*

MATERIALS

❋

- Basic sewing equipment
- Sewing machine
- 1¾ yards of lining fabric, 45 inches wide
- ¾ yard of front fabric, 45 inches wide
- ¾ yard of fusible interfacing, 45 inches wide
- Matching sewing thread
- Five self-cover buttons
- Tailor's chalk or basting thread
- Vest patterns in the correct size – 1 front, 1 back, 1 belt
- Unless otherwise stated, *all* fabric should be pinned and basted before machine stitching, and *all* seams should be pressed open.
- All seam allowances are ⅝ inch

MAKING A VEST BLOCK PATTERN

1 Select the relevant pieces for the vest you want to make. You will need to copy the front and back, and possibly features such as belts, loops, or pockets.

2 To enlarge the pattern you could use a photocopier, but it can also be done on graph paper (see page 107). You can easily alter the pattern by adding a little extra length at the shoulder seam, or at the sides.

3 On a large sheet of paper, draw a grid of equal squares. Tape a sheet of tracing paper over the grid and copy the pattern pieces shown in the book, square for square. Cut out the front and back pattern pieces.

4 To avoid wasting fabric, lay the pattern pieces on newspaper, draw around them, and cut them out, then pin together a paper version of your vest and try it on to see if the shoulders, side seams, or armholes need adjusting.

5 If you plan to use the pattern several times, it is worth cutting a stronger template out of cardboard.

TO FINISH

SOME PROJECTS INVOLVE MARKING THE FRONTS ONLY BUT NOT CUTTING THEM OUT UNTIL THE DECORATION HAS BEEN APPLIED, SO CHECK THE INSTRUCTIONS BEFORE YOU BEGIN.

mark around all the sides and the darts. Remove the pattern piece, and cut out the front panels. Lay the center back edge of the back pattern against the fold of the fabric, mark around, and cut out the back piece.

1 Fold the right sides of the fabric together, lay the front pattern on the fabric, parallel to the edges, and with chalk or basting thread

2 Cut two more fronts and a back pattern piece from the lining fabric as for the main fabric. Mark the darts. Cut two interfacings using the front pattern piece, again marking the darts. Cut two belt pieces.

3 Iron interfacing to the back side of the decorated front to stiffen it. Set the machine for straight stitch with a stitch length of 3 or 4. Stitch the darts on the front panels and the lining fronts.

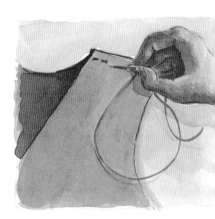

4 Baste and stitch the shoulder seams together for the front and back fabric panels. Then baste and stitch the lining in the same way. Press all seams and darts.

5 Make the belt by folding each piece in half, lengthwise, stitching one short edge and the long edge. Press, turn right side out, press again.

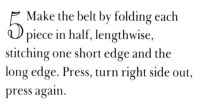

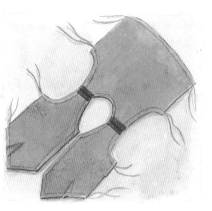

6 Lay the fabric and lining pieces right sides together on a flat surface and pin all around the edges, except for the side seams between the armhole and the lower edge. Baste, then stitch all seams, leaving the sides open.

7 Clip into the armhole curves and remove any bulk at seams. Clip excess fabric from the corners. Press seams.

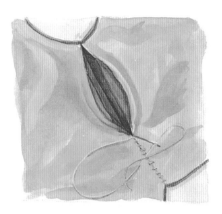

9 Place the fabric with side seams right sides together and pin from the armhole to the lower edge, then stitch. Press the lining side seam edges ⅝ inch to the inside, pin together, and overcast neatly to conceal the raw edges inside.

11 Buttonholes can be made by using either a programmed machine stitch or zigzag stitch, or handsew them using buttonhole stitch. Remember that you do not cut the buttonhole slit until the stitching is finished. Practice on a spare piece of fabric first. The buttonhole should be slightly larger than the finished size of the button. You can cover the buttons with matching fabric and attach to the opposite front to correspond with the buttonholes. Alternatively, use purchased buttons.

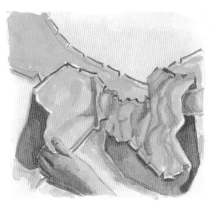

8 Turn the vest right side out by pulling the fronts through the shoulder tunnel and out through the open side edge of the back. Press carefully all around the edges.

10 Fold the raw belt edges under ⅝ inch and press. Place on the vest back approximately 10 inches from each side seam. Each belt piece (tier) should face the edge. Topstitch a square on each belt piece to anchor it in place. The ties are knotted together when the vest is worn.

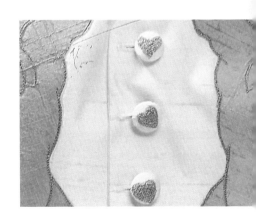

VARIOUS FEATURES CAN BE ADDED TO A VEST SUCH AS A HALF-BELT, SIDE VENTS, POCKETS, OR A COLLAR. TRADITIONALLY THE REPOSITORY FOR THE GOLD FOB WATCH, POCKETS ARE NOW OFTEN FOR DECORATION ONLY AND MAY JUST BE FALSE FLAPS OR PIPED EDGING. WHEN THE VEST IS WORN OVER A SHIRT, A COLLAR SITS OUTSIDE IT. BUT FOR WEARING AS A FASHION GARMENT IN ITS OWN RIGHT, A VEST CAN BE FINISHED WITH AN ATTACHED COLLAR MADE IN A MATCHING OR CONTRASTING FABRIC.

ADDITIONAL FEATURES

✿   ✿   ✿   ✿   ✿   ✿   ✿   ✿   ✿   ✿   ✿   ✿   ✿   ✿   ✿   ✿

Pockets can be a useful decorative feature, but the type should be selected carefully to suit the decorative technique used. Patch pockets and false flaps are easy to attach, but piped pockets should not be attempted on bulky fabrics or those that have machine embroidery, embossed stenciling, appliqué or patchwork, as it would be very difficult to achieve a flat, neat finish. False pockets for vests are best made from a single layer of fabric as the weight of a real pocket will affect the way the front panels hang. But stronger fabrics and lined vests can have real pouched pockets, provided the opening is double stitched to avoid stretching or splitting when in use.

A collar can finish a vest nicely. Vests were commonly worn over shirts, with the shirt collar sitting outside. So to achieve this look when wearing a vest on its own, you may want to attach a collar — permanently, or with easily removable slipstitching or fastenings. Matching or contrasting fabrics can be equally effective.

POCKETS

TO MAKE A PIPED POCKET, YOU WILL NEED TWO MATCHING FABRIC STRIPS. THE POCKET ITSELF IS ACTUALLY A FLAT ENVELOPE ATTACHED TO THE WRONG SIDE OF THE GARMENT.

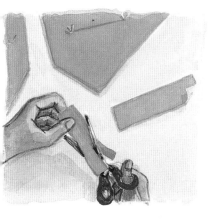

1 Mark the pocket opening on the right side of the fabric, then cut two strips of fabric 1¼ inches wide and at least 2 inches longer than the pocket opening. Iron fusible web onto the wrong side of each strip and peel off the paper backing. Fold each strip in half, bonded sides together, and press with an iron to bond them together. Trim the strip to twice the required width of the finished piping.

2 Cut pieces of iron-on interfacing 2 inches wide and 1½ inches longer than the pocket slit marks and iron them onto the wrong side of the vest over the pocket slit marks.

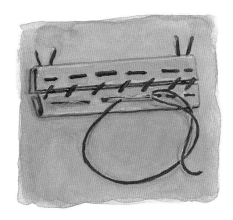

3 On the right side of the fabric, center the piping strips along the line for the opening. Baste them into position and then baste down the raw edges.

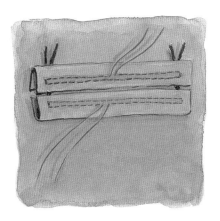

4 Machine-stitch back and forth along the center between the two rows of piping, starting and finishing at the center point to give a double row of stitches close together. Remove all basting threads. Turn the garment wrong side out and slit carefully between the two rows of machine stitching to within ⅜ inch at each end.

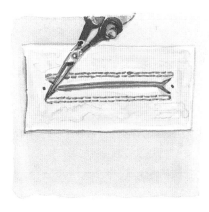

5 Snip carefully into the corners.

6 Push the piping strips through to the wrong side, and hold them in place by overcasting with basting stitches on the right side. Fold back the triangles of fabric at each end and press the piping flat. On the right side of the pocket opening, stab stitch or machine stitch across the slit ends, or machine stitch all around the opening. This will hold the piping flat.

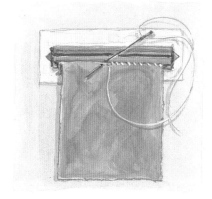

7 Cut two pieces of fabric or lining 1¼ inches shorter than the length of piping and approximately 6 inches deep. Fold in the raw edge of one piece and hem it to the lower piping, facing right side up. With right sides facing, place the second piece of fabric even with the upper piping. Stitch it to the piping by hand or by machine using a piping foot.

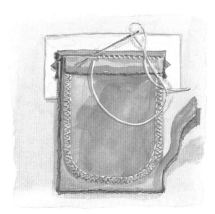

8 Baste the two pocket pieces together. Mark the outline of the pocket, curving the corners. Stitch around the edge, then turn it inside out and zigzag stitch around the raw edges to finish. Make the second pocket to match.

COLLARS

A COLLAR CAN BE THE FOCAL POINT OF A GARMENT, AND IT SHOULD BE MADE WITH CARE FOR A PROFESSIONAL RESULT. ALL COLLARS REQUIRE INTERFACING, EITHER THROUGHOUT OR IN CERTAIN AREAS FOR STRENGTH AND DEFINITION. USE THE CORRECT WEIGHT OF INTERFACING FOR THE FABRIC. LIGHTWEIGHT FABRICS ARE SUITABLE FOR BOTH FRONT AND BACK OF A COLLAR. BULKY FABRICS SUCH AS THICK WOOL, VELVET, OR FUR SHOULD HAVE A BACKING MADE OF LINING MATERIAL. THE FOLLOWING INSTRUCTIONS SHOW HOW TO ATTACH A SHAWL COLLAR.

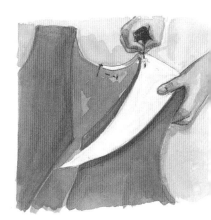

1 Trace the paper pattern on page 126 and pin it in place on the vest. Lengthen or shorten it as necessary at this stage. The center back collar line should meet the center back line of the vest. When fitted, unpin the pattern.

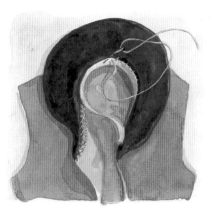

2 Lay the corrected collar pattern on top of the fabric folded with right sides together. Pin the pattern in place and cut around it. Cut matching pieces of interfacing, and lining if required. Trim off ½ inch all around the interfacing.

4 Place backing and front fabric, right sides together, then pin, baste, and stitch the outer collar edge, leaving a ⅝-inch seam allowance. Trim away excess bulk from center seams, then clip small triangular areas from the seam allowance, snipping close to but not right up to the stitching line. This will ensure the curved edge lies flat. Turn collar right side out and press flat.

6 Fold over the fabric collar and hand stitch it in place over the backing using a small herringbone stitch. Hand stitch bias binding over the top of the seam to cover all edges.

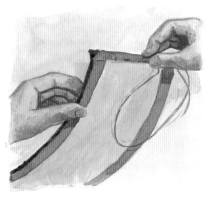

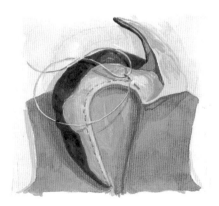

3 Iron the interfacing onto the fabric. Pin the collar right sides together along the short edge. Baste, then stitch together, leaving a ⅝-inch seam allowance. Press the seam open. Repeat this to make the collar lining piece from the same fabric, or lining material.

5 Pin the raw backing edge of the collar to the neck edge of the vest, right sides together. Baste and machine stitch, using a ⅝-inch seam allowance. Zigzag the raw edges to prevent fraying.

BUTTONS OR FASTENINGS ADD THE FINISHING TOUCHES TO YOUR VEST AND CAN BE AN IMPORTANT FEATURE. IT IS NOT ALWAYS NECESSARY TO MAKE CORRESPONDING BUTTONHOLES AS THE GARMENT CAN BE FASTENED BY OTHER, SIMPLER BUT INVISIBLE MEANS, SUCH AS PATENT FASTENERS. ZIPPERS, FROG FASTENERS, BUCKLES, AND BOWS ARE ALL POSSIBLE DECORATIVE ALTERNATIVES TO BUTTONS.

FASTENINGS

✸ ✸ ✸ ✸ ✸ ✸ ✸ ✸ ✸ ✸ ✸ ✸ ✸ ✸ ✸ ✸

After designing and decorating your own vest, it can be fun to make a matching set of buttons. Self-cover button sets, available in all sizes from notions counters, provide endless opportunities. All you need is small circles of fabric to cover the metal base; then you snap on the metal backing piece and the button is ready to sew on. You can decorate your fabric in dozens of different ways, from machine embroidery to fabric painting, or simply use key motifs selected from a patterned fabric. On a heavily decorated vest, plain covered buttons in a coordinating color will work equally well.

Collecting buttons is a fascinating hobby and you may find just the ones for your vest. You might even plan a whole new design around a rather special set of buttons.

Making your own buttons from scratch is quite easy, using one of the new oven-hardened modeling clays which come in a wide choice of colors. You will quickly learn how to mix and blend the colors and create amazing patterns, and they can be made into interesting shapes such as hearts, flowers, animals, or butterflies. To finish the whole outfit, you could make a matching pair of earrings, too.

HEART BUTTONS

MACHINE-EMBROIDERED FABRIC HAS BEEN CUT AWAY TO REVEAL A HEART IN A CONTRASTING COLOR. THIS DESIGN WILL SUIT ANY PLAIN VEST.

1 Set the machine for embroidery. Fill the bobbin with lime thread. Use the gold thread on the top.

2 Stretch the two pieces of fabric into the hoop with the green fabric uppermost. Lay a cardboard template on the fabric and trace around it using chalk or a pen. Repeat across the fabric for the required number of buttons.

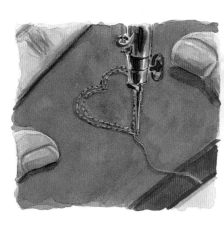

3 Begin by embroidering around the heart three times, then scroll lacy detail around the heart.

4 Embroider all the circles, remove the fabric from the hoop, and using embroidery scissors, snip away the inside of the heart, *only* removing the green fabric, leaving the pink intact. Trim around the cutting edge. Cover the metal buttons as directed by the manufacturer.

BEADED BUTTONS

ATTACH GLITTERING BEADS TO BUTTONS FOR A SPARKLY LOOK SUITABLE FOR A PARTY OUTFIT.

1 Using a cardboard template, trace the shape onto the fabric for the required number of buttons. Trim around the cutting edge and cover the button bases.

2 Place a dot of glue on the center of the button and on the base of the silver flower. Glue the gold sequin on top, then evenly space the bugle beads around the edge. Leave to set.

ROSEBUD BUTTONS

THESE BUTTONS COULD BE USED TO DECORATE THE ROSEBUD VEST FEATURED ON PAGE 64 OR TO ADD A FEMININE TOUCH TO A PLAIN VEST.

1 Using a cardboard template, trace the shape onto the fabric for the required amount of buttons. Trim around the cutting edge and cover the button bases.

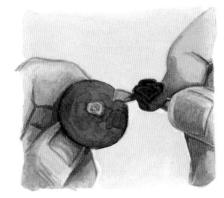

2 Place a dot of glue in the center of the button and one on the base of the rosebud. Press gently together until the glue is set and the bud firmly attached.

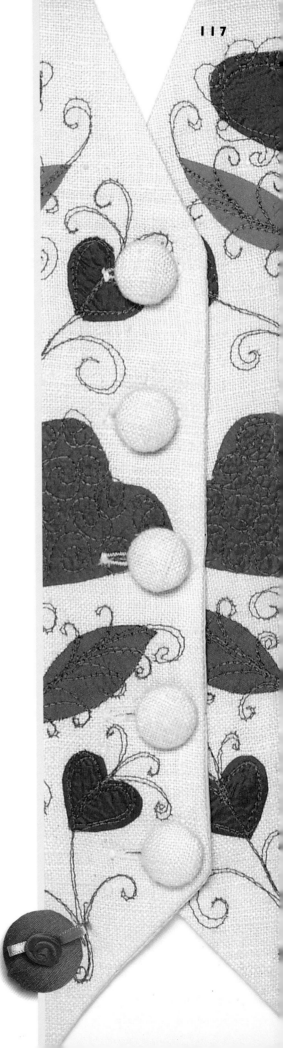

PATTERNS

❅ ❅ ❅ ❅ ❅ ❅ ❅

The patterns given on pages 118–26 include a standard ladies' (chest size 34–36 inches), a standard mens' (chest size 38–40 inches) and some that are specific to a particular project. Certain designs have different shapes so check the patterns carefully before you begin. Scale up the patterns by 262 per cent, using either the photocopy or grid method as described on page 109. If using the grid method your new enlarged square size should be 1 inch. Make up the pattern in paper, pinning it in place to insure a good fit. To adjust, add or subtract width at the sides (remember there are tiers at the back which will draw the waistcoat in). If the vest is too long you can trim the shoulder seam by up to 1 inch or you can trim the bottom edge. You will now have a personal vest pattern.

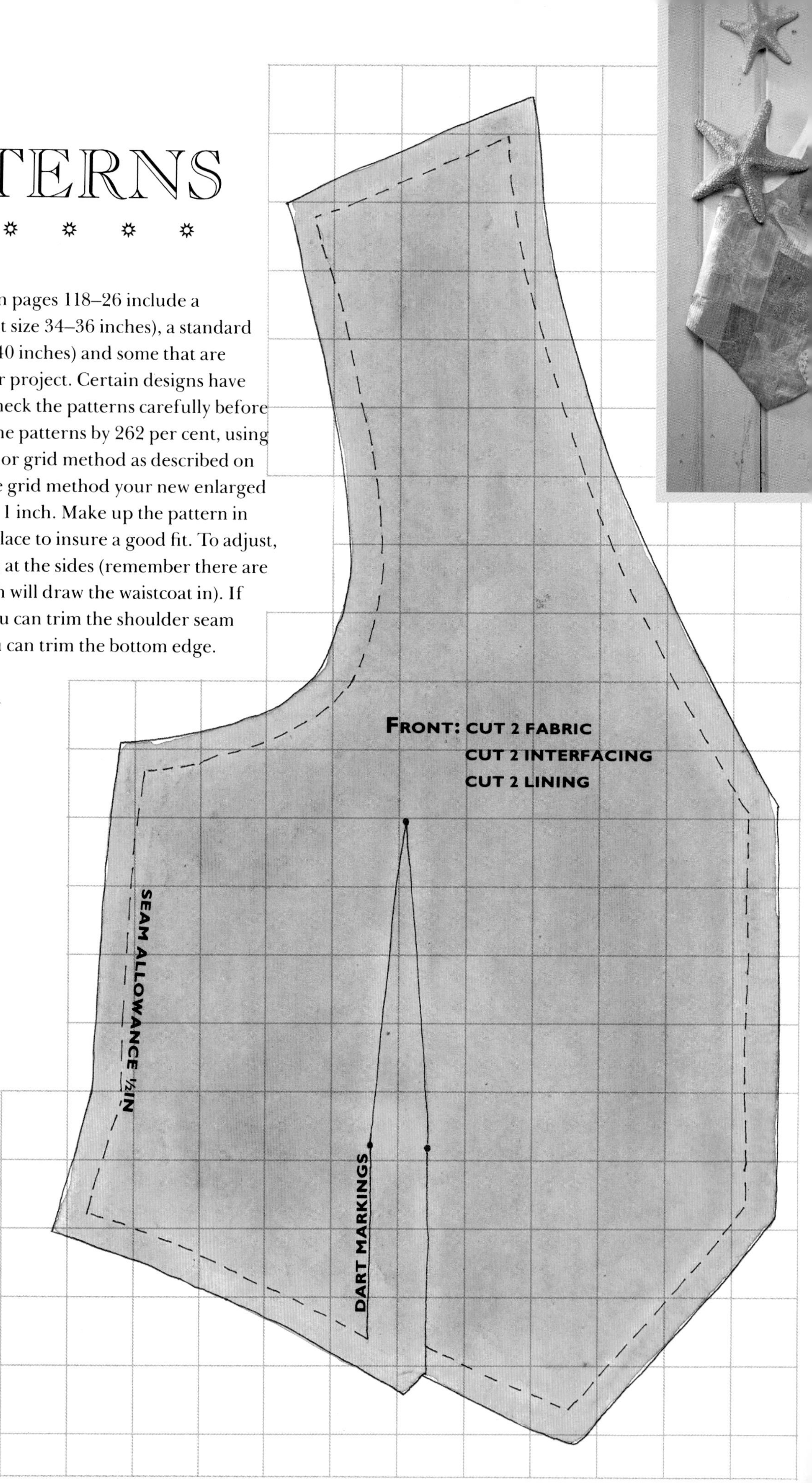

FRONT: CUT 2 FABRIC
CUT 2 INTERFACING
CUT 2 LINING

SEAM ALLOWANCE ½IN

DART MARKINGS

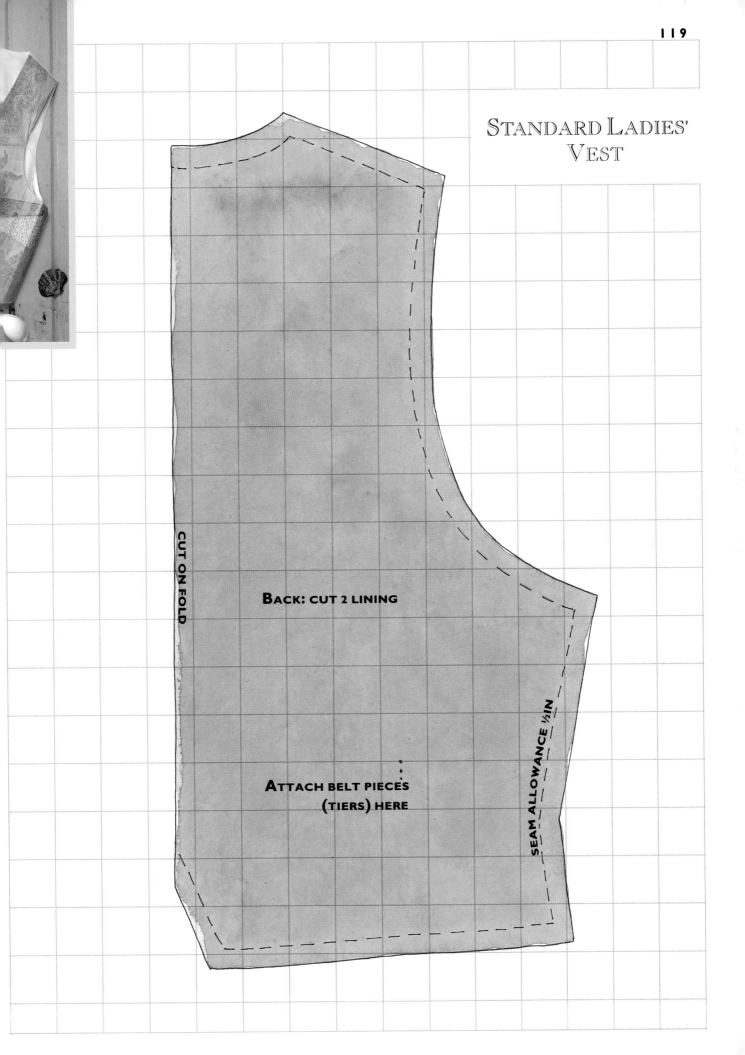

STANDARD LADIES'
VEST

CUT ON FOLD

BACK: CUT 2 LINING

**ATTACH BELT PIECES
(TIERS) HERE**

SEAM ALLOWANCE ½IN

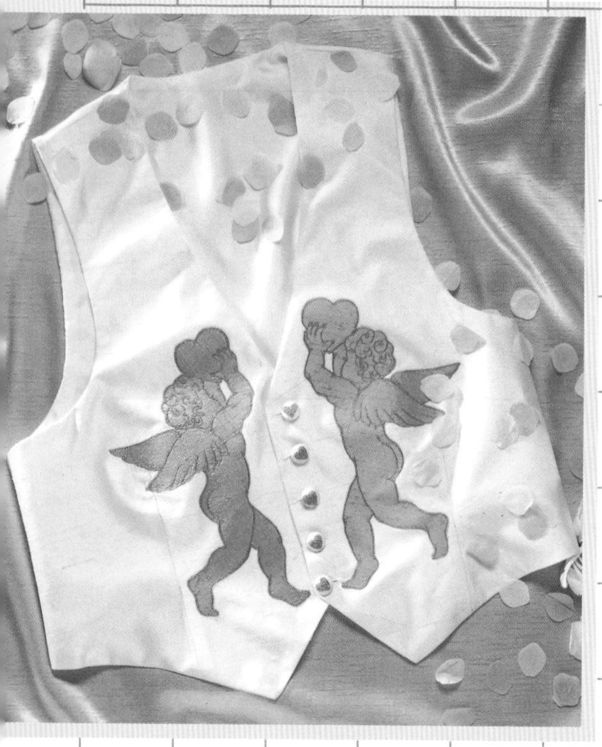

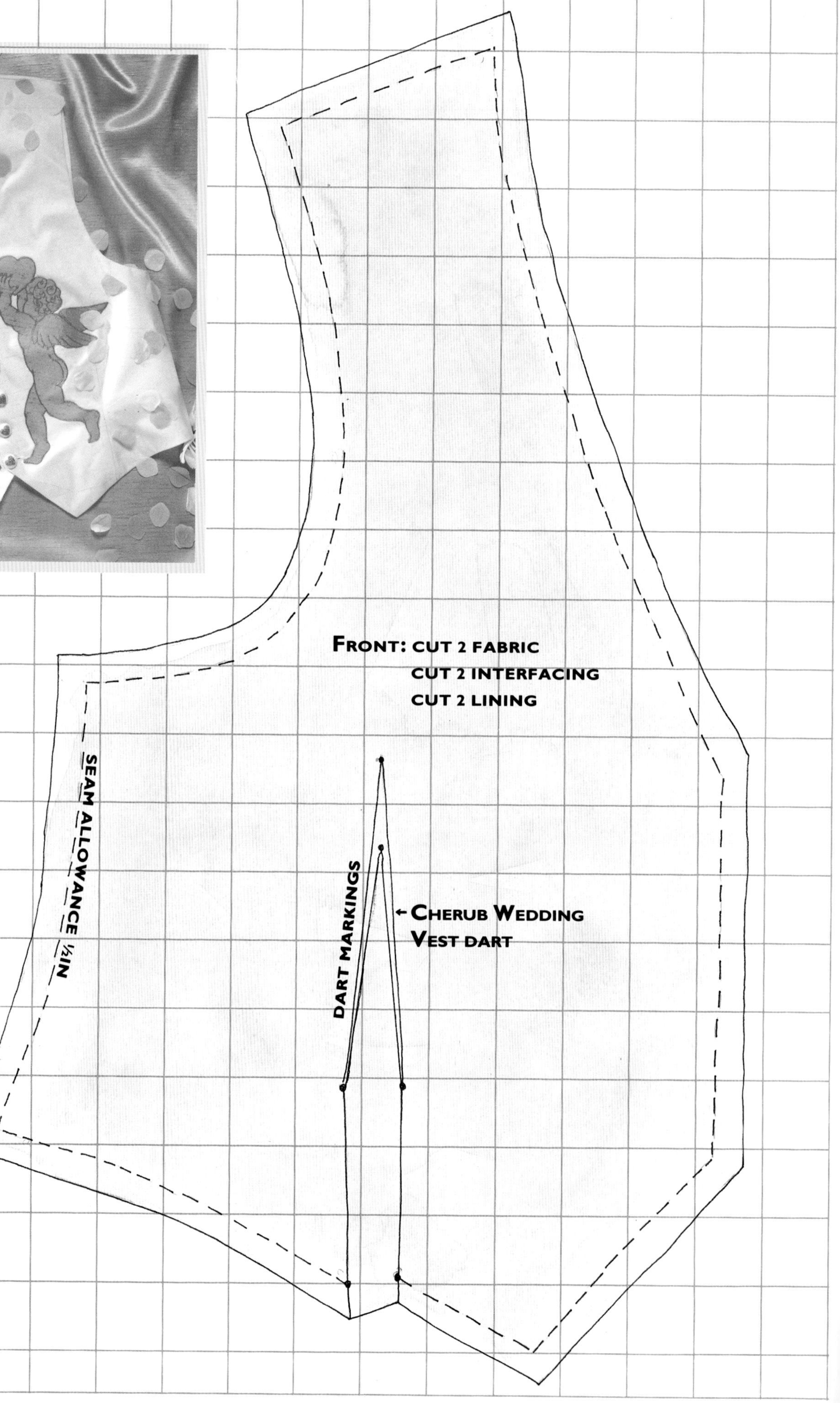

FRONT: CUT 2 FABRIC
CUT 2 INTERFACING
CUT 2 LINING

SEAM ALLOWANCE ½IN

DART MARKINGS

← **CHERUB WEDDING VEST DART**

STANDARD MENS'
VEST

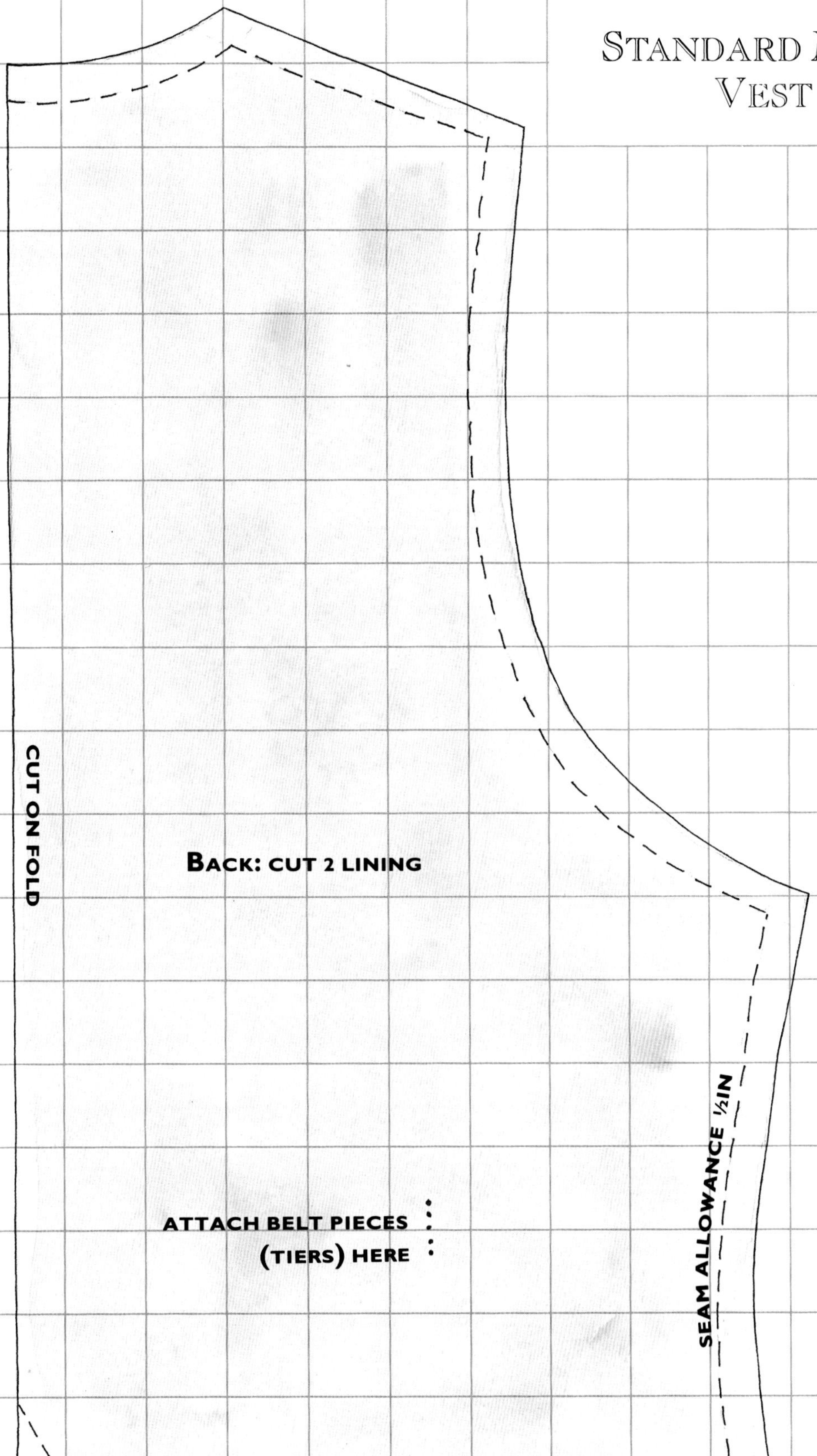

CUT ON FOLD

BACK: CUT 2 LINING

SEAM ALLOWANCE ½IN

ATTACH BELT PIECES
(TIERS) HERE

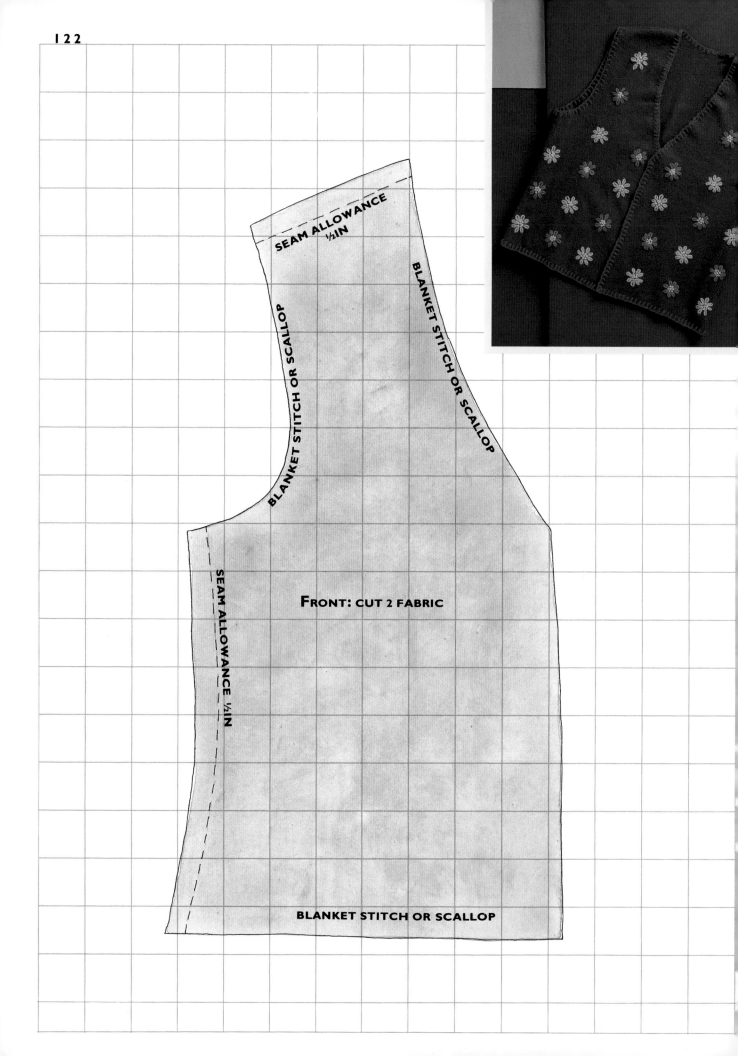

SEAM ALLOWANCE ½IN

BLANKET STITCH OR SCALLOP

BLANKET STITCH OR SCALLOP

SEAM ALLOWANCE ½IN

FRONT: CUT 2 FABRIC

BLANKET STITCH OR SCALLOP

MEXICAN FELT
VEST AND
SIMPLE SUMMER
VEST

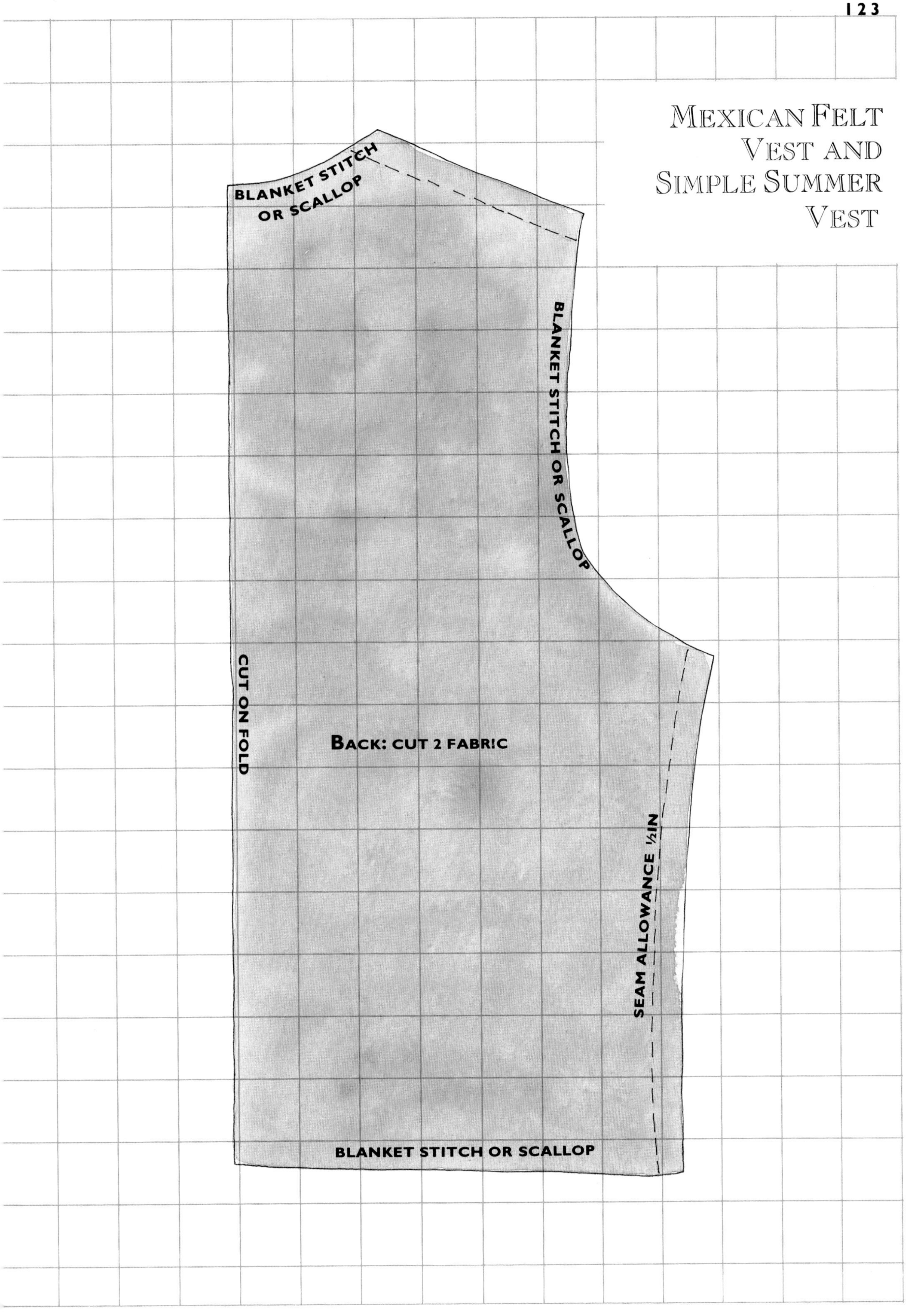

BLANKET STITCH
OR SCALLOP

BLANKET STITCH OR SCALLOP

CUT ON FOLD

BACK: CUT 2 FABRIC

SEAM ALLOWANCE ½IN

BLANKET STITCH OR SCALLOP

FRONT: CUT 2 FABRIC
CUT 2 INTERFACING
CUT 2 LINING

SEAM ALLOWANCE ½IN

DART MARKINGS

ROMANTIC
VELVET
FISH VEST

CUT ON FOLD

BACK: CUT 2 LINING

SEAM ALLOWANCE ½IN

FUN FUR COLLAR

ADD OR TAKE AWAY FABRIC FROM HERE

+ OR

KEEP THIS PANEL

THE SAME

OR +

STANDARD LADIES' AND MENS' BELT (TIERS)

enlarge by 190 per cent

CUT 2 LINING

POCKET BAG

CUT 2 FABRIC
CUT 2 BONDING

CUT 2 LINING

INDEX

CREDITS

The author would like to thank her parents and husband for their support. Also, thanks to Alistair McAuley, Carol Armour and Louise Brown for their special help.

Quarto Publishing would like to thank all the makers who contributed to the book:

Alison Bell, Arran Fine Art Silks, 4 Lakeside Place, Shiskine, Isle of Arran KA27 8EP
Pookie Blezard, Pazuki, 2 Beverley Gardens, London SW13 0LZ
Gilda Brown and **Shelagh O'Gorman,** 27 Flambard Rd, Harrow, Middlesex HA1 2NB
Toria Chaumeton, Torbagz Clothing Company, Unit 1.11b, Belgravia Workshops, 157–163 Marlborough Rd, London N19 4NF
Catherine Crowther, The Studio, Lovingtons, Great Yeldham, Halstead, Essex CO9 4HP
Sally Cunningham, 21 Solent Way, Alverstoke, Hampshire PO12 2NR
Jacqueline Farrell Textiles, The Old Church Studios, 92 Raeberry St, Glasgow G20 6EG
Judith Gait, St. Mary's Cottage, Hemington, Bath BA3 5XX
Gilbey's Waistcoat Gallery, 2 New Burlington Place, Savile Row, London W1
Deborah Gonet, 207b Chevening Rd, Queens Park, London NW6 6DT
Jo Hall, 6 Gilmore Drive, Prestwich, Manchester M25 5LB
Kate Haynes, 37 Parchment St, Winchester, Hants SO23 8BA
Caroline Keill, 86a Lorne Rd, London E7 0LL
Elspeth Kemp, 28 St Leonards Rd, Bangeo, Hertford, Herts SG14 3JW

Gaynor Kirby, Lesta Villa, Seaton Ross, York YO4 4LU
Rosemary MacCarthy Morrogh, 14 Marlborough Rd, Glenageary, Co. Dublin, Ireland
Liz McLean McKay, 24 Pauline Ave, Toronto, Canada/80 Fulwood Ave, Knightswood, Glasgow
Susie Moore, Waisted Art, 306 Hursley Rd, Chandlers Ford, Eastleigh, Hampshire SO5 1PF
Vera Morgan, 5 Penian, Deganwy, Llandudno, Gwynedd, North Wales LL30 1PE
Janet and Roger Quilter, Penpompren, Rhydcymerau, Nr. Landeilo, Dyfed SA19 7PP
Charles Robertson, 3 Syndenham Rd, Glasgow
Georgina von Etzdorf, 50 Burlington Arcade, London W1V 9AE

Quarto would also like to thank **Coats Crafts UK,** PO Box, McMullen Rd, Darlington, Co. Durham, DL1 1YQ for allowing us to use their pattern leaflet no. 4820 for the Sunflower Knit Vest (pages 36–9) and for sponsorship of thread and fabric for the Rosebud Cross-stitch Vest (pages 64–7).

Index by Dorothy Frame